Be A Citrix Hero

Rescue Your Users from Poor Performance & Advance Your Career

By D.J. Eshelman

Be A Citrix Hero: Rescue Your Users from Poor Performance & Advance Your Career

ISBN: 978-1-952105-09-8

Ver 3.6 (LuLu)

Introduction- Why I Am Doing This

Between 2017 and 2018, I decided to catalog the recommendations I was making as a Citrix Consultant. I was making these recommendations for companies paying well over $15,000 for me to be there, typically for a week-long assessment.

The pattern I saw repeatedly was that I tended to be making the same recommendations very frequently.

This tells me that this is information that the community absolutely needs!

Now, what was troubling about this was that this is not proprietary information! In fact, this is *all* freely available information! The problem is that there is a lot of information out there. A lot of distractions.

What was missing was guidance and context.

In hero stories, there is always a guide. They may not be the hero. Maybe they were once the hero. Maybe they are a 12-year-old kid that helps put things in perspective. After over 20 years at this, I'm hanging up my cape for a little while so I can help YOU learn to be the hero.

I have compiled these recommendations to those that repeat themselves most often among more than 350 individual recommendations from assessments over the past few years. I took the top of the stack that I felt would yield the highest results for you with the least effort – in other words- the actions you could take to become the Citrix Hero!

But more than that, I see a lot of pain out there. Many people I meet are not confident about Citrix. They spend late nights trying to deal with problems that could have been avoided. They wonder about their job future. I think that's a shame. I decided to do something about it. That is why I expanded my recommendations with additional context, so you understand the deeper question of WHY they are leading practices.

There are many elements to deploying Citrix technologies and many blogs out there that offer a great many ways to fine tune your environment. I am by no means saying that they are not valid or that you shouldn't consider them. What I am categorizing here are the highest-impact strategies, the ones that cost the least to deploy (especially in terms of effort) and have the highest results. What is unique about this book and its companion guide is that I'm going into much more detail than usual. I include a lot of related recommendations that I found were too much for blogs and freebies. They could merit their own chapter at times. So, I did just that. I started with three chapters, 10,000 words and went from there. What you hold in your hand (or screen) is a result of 8 months of lessons given to the paying members of the Citrix Hero community, put into written form.

Because in many cases just text on a page isn't adequate, I have included additional resources and guides for you with this book. As you read, I will send you opportunities to get in deeper with video lessons and an option to view the original video recordings from these lessons as well as an online video course with downloadable guides. I also, on occasion, update information within the book or give additional resources as they pertain to being a successful Citrix Hero, directly to your email inbox.

You can register for these companion materials by visiting

https://ctxpro.com/herobonus7

I encourage you not just to check your environment for these leading practices but, more importantly, to understand WHY they are considered leading practices and APPLY them to your environment.

I hope you not only benefit from these tips but that you become known in your company as...

The Citrix Hero.

How to Use This Guide

This reference is intended as a teaching tool to help you think as a consultant would. Amid your busy schedule (and let's be honest, life), I hope that you'll take the time to learn not just the technology but the underlying purpose behind it.

Scoring

I use a scoring system for each topic's overall recommendation so you can see at a glance:

- The overall importance to your company leadership
- The level of impact on your users
- How much of a security impact the topic involves
- How difficult the solution is to implement (the skill level involved)

Layers

I use a system of defining the focus areas for each recommendation called Layers. This system is similar (nearly the same) as Citrix uses with the following layers:

- **Business** (how the solution meets the business objectives of the company)
- **User** (the needs, applications, devices, and ways users work)
- **Access** (how users get information and applications)
- **Resource** (the applications, desktops and documents and how they are structured)
- **Control** (Services, Policies and back-end configurations that control resources and access)
- **Platform / Cloud** (The physical and virtual host, hypervisor, network, storage, and other considerations)
- **Security** (the methods by which information will stay under corporate control, etc.)
- **Operations** (The team, tools and other techniques used to maintain the environment)

Success Lanes

I'll also include a skills inventory system that aligns with my other training and membership programs. Here's how this works. My members learn within four primary areas that I call Success Lanes.

- **Understand** (knowing what Citrix solutions are and why they are important)
- **Maintain** (managing the day-to-day operations for Citrix technology)
- **Build** (Engineers and others tasked with making changes or building new environments)
- **Design** (persons tasked with the guidance and overall planning for Citrix technology)

Where appropriate, I'll also include any prerequisite knowledge and links for each tip.

Methodology

I use a specific Methodology in IT Services (and beyond) that I call the "riskLESS" Methodology. It uses four iterative phases to reduce risk in projects and in day-to-day operations. Each phase indicates an overall goal to achieve that can be returned to within a project cycle or day to day operations.

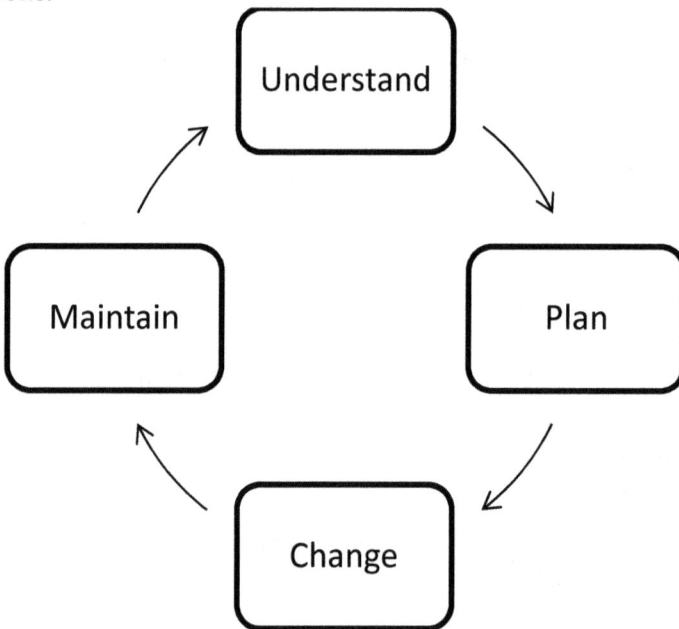

Figure 1: DJ's riskLESS Methodology

Rescue Your Users from Poor Performance & Advance Your Career

- ***Understand.*** Ensuring that the business objectives, risks, and any problems are understood by all parties before any work is done. This can include a full infrastructure assessment, a discovery meeting or even in some cases just being notified of a bug fix that needs to be addressed.
- ***Plan.*** Design to meet the requirements, then coordinate resources, schedules and expectations of each person involved.
- ***Change.*** Execution of the changes needed until the result (for example, a steady state) is achieved.
- ***Maintain.*** Monitoring and administration of the system with the goal of keeping stability and continually meeting any objectives. This includes identifying when it is necessary to begin the cycle over again with *Understand*.

Links

New in this edition: I've listened to your feedback and I agree! To make things look better on the page, easier to read, and deal with broken web links, I am including a quick link table at https://ctxpro.com/CHlinks. Here's how it works. Each link in the book will have a link number. For example if you want link #10, use the format https://ctxpro.com/CHlinks/#10

Much easier than typing in the whole link manually I hope!

I'll also include a table of all the links in the Appendix for your reference.

Also, if you are reading the electronic version, the reference will be clickable, just watch for the underlined text.

But Wait, There's More!

Good news for this 2020 edition! I have decided to include an extended discussion about this and an excerpt from my upcoming book "Just Do THIS" in the Bonus Chapter on Change Management!

If you need help, the Citrix Hero community is here for you. You can become a member at https://community.citrixhero.com [https://ctxpro.com/CHlinks/#1] or email me at CoachDJ@CTXPro.com for a consultation.

Contents

Chapter 1: Windows OS Tuning

It is one of the most popular web searches regarding Citrix.

It is one of the most well-documented and blogged about topics.

Yet I still manage to find this one ignored recommendation more than any other. This truly amazes me because I think this one thing, when properly implemented, can save companies in some cases tens of thousands of dollars every year- and the information on how to do so is free and has been for more than a decade!

So why isn't this being done? Because in the 'click next, next, next' nature of install in the modern End User Computing (EUC) world, it is becoming so easy to install components that those without experience are now able to install and run with Citrix effectively. As you'll see later, simply making another thing to click "next" for would be risky for Citrix to do, even with the current tools available. Why?

This first big superpower involves overcoming limitations in the default settings of the Microsoft Operating system.

Layers	• **Resource**
Success Lanes	• Design • Build
Prerequisites	• Windows Desktop and Server OS Knowledge • Image Deployment Design
Importance	🎸 🎸 🎸 🎸 🎸
User Impact	🎸 🎸 🎸 🎸 🎸
Security Impact	🎸 🎸
Difficulty	🎸 🎸

The #1 Culprit of Bad Performance: Operating System Defaults

Did you know that the 'out of the box' configuration for every Microsoft OS is NOT optimized for virtual delivery? Microsoft builds the operating system for compatibility, not performance.

Why? It mostly has to do with the number of background services and tasks that ship with Windows. Microsoft's intention is good. It serves a broader range of needs. Moreover, it is better to have these "on" by default rather than try to make the thousands of mechanisms to detect when a service is appropriate.

For example, this is why you'll see Bluetooth services on server OS on a Virtual Machine (VM) when you would clearly not need it. You're still installing from the same medium and Microsoft hasn't yet made a way to disable these unneeded services even in these obvious scenarios.

Microsoft assumes YOU will fine-tune the services and settings for your use case!

On Microsoft's website you will find a guide for basic recommendations for tuning VDI [https://ctxpro.com/CHlinks/#2].

Yet, with each release of the Operating system (or in the case of Windows 10, each iteration or build), it seems the amount of resources (CPU, Memory, IO) increases… all because there are so many things running in the background. YOUR JOB is to figure out which of these is beneficial and which ones are not in a Virtual Environment.

Leaving default services (that do not need to be running) as active uses CPU, Memory & IO without giving any benefit to your company. It is wasteful, and some may say shameful. Okay, I'm saying it: it's shameful.

To make things worse- many of the default Registry settings and buried background scheduled tasks can also tax or ultimately hinder proper operations in a virtual space.

Here are some considerations:

Are you running a Virtual Machine? You probably are, but it is worth exploring the implications here. For example- if virtual, you won't have attached peripherals. So, a way to optimize right away is to make sure that services that support these are not in use (Wireless, Bluetooth, etc.)

Is your machine running on a SAN? Quite often, a traditional VM running on a SAN will be using SSDs. The extra capability there is excellent, but in traditional cases (exceptions will be discussed later in this chapter), performance may be degraded by several VMs running defragmentation (Microsoft now refers to this generally as 'optimization'), and the life of the SSDs is reduced… with minimal positive impact on user experience. The same goes for those on hyper-converged architecture – rearranging blocks isn't always needed (exceptions exist with PVS, but we'll talk about that later).

Are your VMs persistent? Some background tasks are a good idea for machines that persist between reboots- but are a horrible idea on VMs that reset upon reboot! It is essential to know and think about these and determine the benefit individually.

KEY CONCEPT: First Do No Harm

Just because I (or some other expert) say you 'should' perform an optimization task… doesn't make it automatically appropriate for you. You MUST do the work of determining which is appropriate in your case. If you're lost or unsure, I would much rather you reach out to the community at https://community.citrixhero.com and ask the question rather than take the risk.

I mentioned the need is increasing. The need may not always show up on an individual VM, but at scale (several or several hundred), VMs can demonstrate an impact from resources being thrown away with no benefit! Recent tests by LoginVSI have proven that Server 2016 is especially bad in this regard- unoptimized VMs can quite literally cost you thousands of dollars because fewer people can be logged into each VM, and fewer people can be hosted on each physical server. Add in the effects of the Meltdown and Spectre remediations, and virtual hosted servers can do far less with the resources available. This means fewer users per blade at scale, which is a huge problem.

HERE'S THE BAD NEWS: IN 2018, MY OBSERVATIONS WERE THAT 90% OF THE COMPANIES I VISITED FOR ASSESSMENTS DID NOT FOLLOW MANY OF THE CITRIX RECOMMENDED GUIDELINES FOR OPTIMIZATION. THE YEAR PRIOR WAS ABOUT 60%. WHEN THESE COMPANIES IMPLEMENTED THE OPTIMIZATION STEPS CORRECTLY, MOST SAW INCREASED USERS PER BLADE OF OVER 30%. ADD IN THE TIPS AND TRICKS I SHARE WITH YOU BELOW, AND YOU'LL BE DRASTICALLY INCREASING THE PERFORMANCE OVERALL!
THE QUESTION BECOMES – WHY ARE THE NUMBER OF COMPANIES DOING THIS DECREASING AND NOT INCREASING?

Needless to say, it matters; however, fixing it is not difficult or expensive. Most tools I talk about here are free!

Bottom line- saving your company several thousand dollars = **#CitrixHero**

Operating System Optimization for Citrix Use Cases

We know we need to optimize the Operating system for remote use, and in some cases, for multi-user uses. The truth is some of these optimizations can be used on the Control Components as well, but for now, we will focus on Resource Components (VDAs).

Server 2016 is in and of itself a challenge in this regard. Testing from LoginVSI [https://ctxpro.com/CHlinks/#3] has indicated that Server 2016 doesn't scale anywhere near as well as Server 2012R2, even when optimized (though when optimized, it is a lot closer.) Sorry folks, this is just the way it is.

But why, DJ? WHY? The answer, painful as it may be, is quite simple and has been true of every iteration of pretty much every operating system ever.

AS THE OPERATING SYSTEM EVOLVES, IT TENDS TO ADD NEW SCHEDULED TASKS, NEW BACKGROUND SERVICES, AND, OF COURSE, NEW EXECUTABLES RUNNING IN THE BACKGROUND UNDER THE 'SYSTEM' CONTEXT.

It means that the optimizations that were done for one OS won't automatically apply to the next version of that same OS. Yet, this is a mistake I see engineers making over and over again- they optimized for Server 2003 this way, registry keys, for example. Then they do the same for 2012R2 -Nothing new… just those older set of optimizations. Then they wonder why they are only getting half of the users on a single server. They wonder why logons suddenly jump to over a minute with this 'latest and greatest' operating system.

News Flash: NEWER DOES NOT MEAN FASTER

Unlike the car industry or even the hardware on which an operating system is executed- an operating system is typically careful to say that you can DO MORE, but if they claim to be FASTER – beware. There are probably provisos and limitations to consider. In over 20 years of doing this work professionally, I have NEVER encountered an OS that was actually faster in measurable metrics of speed than its predecessor was. Now, productivity and user experience may be improved. After all, when was the last time you booted up Windows 3.1 and tried to do anything productive? We have come a long way in terms of productivity and experience. However, put a newer OS on the same hardware as the previous, and you will rarely get anywhere near as fast of responsiveness. Yet, you may be able to run far more users at once because of more efficient memory processing. So the tradeoff works – but DO NOT fall into the trap of believing or telling management that the new OS will be faster. Even if you can track down and disable every unneeded service, tune every setting and spend months optimizing - the reality is that the perceived speed of metrics like login times may still lag behind what they had   before.
Pro Tip: Sell the Benefits of running a new OS that are real and be upfront that the cost of those new benefits may be in aspects of the experience that are different. Let me give you an example.

I recently helped an organization upgrade from Windows 7 to Windows 10 LTSB. I let them know that the login times would probably increase by about 10 seconds. However, once the desktop loaded app launches and multitasking would lead to more productivity once users learned how to utilize the new OS properly. When management saw the true productivity benefits, they didn't care that the login times were slightly different. And the reality is, users thought it *was* faster. I think it was because it looked new.

Before We Begin

I assume that for all of these improvements that you are testing, making backups, and never EVER placing untested optimizations in production!

All of the optimizations I discuss are mostly free but may be subject to specific usage licensing and caveats. It is your responsibility to read the agreements before you run the tools!

I'm going to assume that you're willing to do some research along with reading this book. At the end of this chapter, I have several articles I want you to read!

Hit the Easy Button: Citrix Optimizer

There are several options these days for scripts and hacks to perform optimizations for you, primary of which is the Citrix Optimizer (CTX224676) [https://ctxpro.com/CHlinks/#4]. Optimizer is a free tool supported by Citrix that automatically detects variations from the recommended tunings and lets you select which ones to apply and which ones not to (for example, on some servers you may want Windows Search to run for Outlook – on others you may not, so optimize and test appropriately).

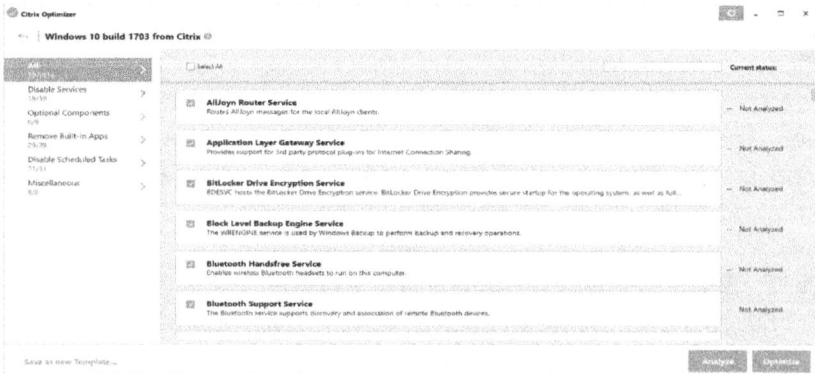

The reality is that merely running this tool will disable unneeded services you didn't even realize were there, remove built-in apps, and set or remove needed key registry settings and scheduled tasks with a few clicks. I love that this has been developed because this used to be either a manual process (which was rarely done) or scripts (which often didn't work, especially with new OS scenarios – thanks, Windows 10...) This application is updated frequently, so you are assured it is going to work. Better than that even, the community is developing templates for better and better optimization scenarios that you can apply automatically. It supports rollback and creating your own templates. In all- what this is doing for free in seconds is what I used to end up charging clients more than $1500 of efforts to complete. You'd be a fool not to take advantage of this!

Don't be a fool – Use the Free Tool! – DJ Eshelman

There are a few caveats:
1. **Take it One Step at a Time**. As you can see in the screenshot above, there are potentially hundreds of optimizations. Some have requested from me a deeper dive into these settings; however, they change too frequently to include in a book. What I am making available is an ongoing and occasionally updated video course on the topic which you'll be able to register for at https://ctxpro.com/herobonus7.
   Generally speaking, I can tell you that Martin Zugec (creator of the Citrix Optimizer tool) and the CTA/CTP groups are continually working to validate these settings. What they've done is created the "Optional Components" section. My suggestion is to validate the base recommendations first, make a backup, then test each of the Optional Components INDIVIDUALLY. Unless directed by a consultant specifically (or you know what you're doing), the components in this section can sometimes even cause VDI to stop working in extreme cases but are suitable for back-end services. As you'll often hear with Citrix Consulting: "It Depends..."
2. **TEST**. Always test before going into production with changes like this. Just because you hear me say to do something great doesn't

mean that every element of it is required for your users. Every use case has little differences that require your attention.

3. **Be careful with specific Optimizer options such as disabling Windows Search**. The Search services may be something your users need for Outlook or other requirements, and their user experience will be diminished without it. In many cases, I find that one image may require services that another does not because of the users logging in and applications they run. Does that mean you should skip both? No, it means you should do the optimization when it is appropriate! Search is an excellent example of an 'expensive' to run service that is valuable to some users (and potentially not to others). So, do your research, segment, and then test!

4. **You *can* run Optimizer on Control servers** (Broker/Controllers, StoreFront, PVS, etc.) but be very aware when you do. Monitor event logs closely, and as always, TEST BEFORE YOU DEPLOY.

Special note here- if you sign up for Citrix Smart Tools, Optimizer Checks can be scheduled for you! Learn more about that and the other system checks at https://ctxpro.com/CHlinks/#5.

PVS Target Device Optimization Tool

I won't linger on this topic a lot, but the very first automatic tool for Citrix VDAs was the PVS Target Device Optimization Tool. The tool is typically run when you first capture a vDisk. However- many people don't realize that the tool can be run AGAIN at any time. There are some caveats, however:

As mentioned before- while disabling Windows Search makes a lot of sense theoretically for PVS workloads, it is a good idea to make sure your apps will not need Search integrated (i.e., Outlook).

Do not confuse Search with the Indexing service

By default, the Optimization Tool will disable Windows Defender. This is not always appropriate, so please be aware!

Additionally, if you are using PVS, there are several other tweaks you can test at CTP Carl Stalhood's site [https://ctxpro.com/CHlinks/#6].

Bonus Optimizations!

Though I don't *always* make these recommendations during my assessments, there are a few additional items that I can't ignore to kick your optimizations into high gear! More settings that, if left at the 'default' setting, hurt you in the long term, especially at scale. Entire books could be written about these topics, and they move so fast with updates that I hesitated to put them here at all. For fast-moving information like this, I do recommend you subscribe at https://community.citrixhero.com to make sure you get up-to-date recommendations of note as they come along from a community of people who care about the same things you do.

Sealing the Deal: Image Creation the Right Way

Using the Windows Cleanup Tool

Every time you make changes and updates to an image, you'll want to reboot at least twice, then run the Windows Cleanup utility (cleanmgr.exe) as an administrator to scan through not only temp files but older updates that no longer need to be there. The process takes quite a while, but it is not uncommon for me to see savings of 2-3 GB by doing this process.

Defragmentation – the Hidden Performance Thief

Another overlooked item, especially with Citrix deployments using a central image (MCS or PVS) and the new Cache in RAM with Overflow to Disk functionality, is defragmentation. 'But I use SSDs,' you say. Good for you. But the Cache in RAM does NOT cache files. It caches *blocks*. If you have fragmented blocks, you can use between 2 and 8 times as much memory to cache. This is because RAM cannot fragment the same way, so if only part of the block is used, too bad: *It still uses the whole block*. When you have made changes to the base image and are getting ready to deploy the new snapshot or vDisk version- Make sure you defragment the image as part of your sealing process.

*Quick tip on PVS- the best way to Defragment is first to clean up the image, then mount the vDisk on the PVS server, where you can defragment it as an attached disk. It is not only faster, but you can defragment files that normally would be in use.

Now, as I mentioned previously, this does not always apply. Here's my general guideline:

Defragment your Base Image before deployment!
Leave everything else alone unless you are running
physical spinning disk on your server or have a specific
reason to keep Defrag running

Using Third-Party Tools

Confession time. I'm often sad when I do a Citrix Consulting gig because I can't recommend Third Party… anything. The reason is solid; Citrix can't support it! That being said, I'd encourage you to test another tool from some people I know and trust. I've used their tools myself, and it works very well. This next tool is one of the best!

BIS-F

BIS-F stands for Base Image Script Framework. The goal was to have a single 'master optimization' script that does everything you should be doing when you 'seal' an image for distribution from either PVS or Machine Creation Services. The list of tasks the script performs is extremely extensive, but a few highlights are making sure Windows activation (KMS) is working correctly, that the drive is optimized (defragmented). The tool is aware of when you are using a non-persistent MCS vs. PVS image and adjusts the strategy accordingly. For example, it can move the ever-increasing number of event logs to your cache drive if you are using PVS.

Another cool feature is running a purge of WEM cache and scanning AntiVirus to mark the drive as safe to a lot of newer programs that can take advantage of this feature (fewer files to scan = better performance). Also, something that is missed all too frequently: .Net Optimization. What this does is initiate a process that often runs at startup. The problem with this in a non-persistent desktop, it would happen every time the image starts up. I have seen this cause massive issues for host CPU in VDI environments. Again- important details that are frequently missed. Thank goodness for scripts!

https://ctxpro.com/CHlinks/#7

VMware Optimizer

The VMware OSOT can optionally run for your workloads (if you are running on VMware only, please). Even though it will say "Horizon View," the reality is that once again- these are *OS optimizations*. As you can imagine, there is a lot of overlap. But if you are running on a VMware host, this is sometimes a good idea. I have NOT tested OSOT on non-VMware hosts, nor do I intend to. It is up to you if you want to try it!

A caveat with OSOT is that it is community-driven, so the odds of getting lousy advice is always real. As always: TEST, TEST and then TEST again! I have recently had instances of engineers using the 'recommended' settings and making their Windows 10 image devoid of a Start Menu, for example. Be careful out there!

Because the updates for this will always be more up to date than this book- I'm asking, *pleading* with you to do two things:

1) Read up on the template settings and consider the implications
2) As above- take each setting one at a time, making backups along the way

You can find the VMWare OST link at https://ctxpro.com/CHlinks/#8

Antivirus Defaults – the Secret Performance Killer

Just like Microsoft's OS settings are made to fit a wide array of solutions 'out of the box,' so also are AntiVirus and Anti-Malware programs. I'm a bit off-topic here, but I make the recommendation enough that I thought I'd go ahead and remind you here. While they are getting better (check out Bitdefender's Hypervisor Introspection with XenServer [https://ctxpro.com/CHlinks/#9] if you have doubts about that), there is still management that needs to be tuned for every anti-malware software.

I encourage you to read Citrix's guidance, which is now in the Tech Zone [https://ctxpro.com/CHlinks/#10]. Also, at a high level, consider these guidelines:

Make sure to exclude Citrix executables

Exclude system files like the page file, print spooler, and cache directories

Set scanning to Write Only, especially on non-persistent MCS and PVS workloads

Do not perform scheduled scans on MCS and PVS workloads (use the BIS-F tool or manually scan before sealing the disk)

There's more here but, but I have one more bonus tip for you.

The Hidden Resource Hog: Ads and Tracking

My friend Dan Allen has been harping on this for a long time, and he's right: with everyone using web browsers all day long, the persistence of advertisements is inevitable even in the workplace. Once again, left to the defaults- the browser will consume all it is told to consume, even ads and tracking. But the good news is there are many ways this can be reduced or eliminated. Reduced to the tune of over 35% less resource consumption according to this LoginVSI whitepaper [https://ctxpro.com/CHlinks/#3].

Here's a list of options, in order of difficulty to deploy:

1. Use a Group Policy Object to enable IE Tracking Protection
2. Use the ublock Browser plugin (trust me when I tell you not to use Adblock plus – uBlock is more efficient as of this writing. However, things change all the time.)
3. Attack the problem via DNS or adjusting the hosts file [https://ctxpro.com/CHlinks/#11]. I'll say again: test this, but I've found it VERY effective. What I find even more effective is using a DNS blocking appliance such as a Pi-Hole, which is a Docker or Raspberry Pi appliance that is updated frequently to block bad DNS actors and ads. My caution with Pi-Hole is that messing with default DNS can also mess with your domain traffic. This really should be the default DNS forwarder, not the DNS handed out by your DHCP servers on the domain, for example.

So, in summary, remember that the default settings are not there for your benefit, but they are there for your safety. They are the compromise draft- the deal no one was happy with but work around it. If you master these, you are on your way to being a #CitrixHero!

Remember, if you want to dive deeper into this topic, I'd like to know! Let me know if you're interested in live Q&A, Online Courses or even webinars on these topics by emailing me at CoachDJ@CTXPro.com

Resources and References

As promised, here are some additional reading and resources on optimizations and general considerations!

- **The Citrix VDI Handbook**: https://ctxpro.com/CHlinks/#12
- **Microsoft RDS-VDI Optimization recommendations**: https://ctxpro.com/CHlinks/#2

- **Windows 10 Optimization Guide PDF** CTX216252: https://ctxpro.com/CHlinks/#13
- **Server 2016 Optimizations from Citrix Architect Daniel Feller**: https://ctxpro.com/CHlinks/#14
- **Windows 8/8.1 and Server 2012/2012 R2 Optimization Guide and Script** (based on a CTX document that is no longer available- Pablo wrote the article for Citrix originally): https://ctxpro.com/CHlinks/#15

Chapter 2: Citrix ADC (NetScaler) Defaults

In the first chapter, we discussed common mistakes that are often made with OS Optimization, or more specifically, a lack thereof because people leave the default settings.

In this chapter- we will talk more about the second big mistake. Similar in the persistence of default settings - but the cost this time is not performance but security!

Those of you following along closely will know that this is not the first time I've talked about problems I see in the Access Layer in general, specifically the NetScaler (now Citrix ADC). One of the biggest problems here is how rapidly the practices change. So much so I'm hesitant to even put anything out there for fear of it being obsolete (as I edit and update this text in 2019 I'm removing references to findings from late 2018 that are already irrelevant). If anyone from Citrix is reading this, please excuse in advance my using "NetScaler" and "Xen" terms. Old habits die hard and when the recommendations were written originally, those were the right terms. So… sorry about that. Let's hope it's another 10 years before we see another massive name change!

Of the reference 350+ individual findings from 2017-2019, there were about 13 commonly repeated findings that were related to the Access Layer. What concerned me most is that when I say 'commonly' I mean they repeated on nearly every assessment. Here are the most common:

- NetScaler Firmware Vulnerable to attack
- Plaintext StoreFront website vulnerable to man-in-the-middle snooping even if secured from NetScaler Gateway front end
- SSL Labs scores not passing; should be an A+
- Other Leading Practices not yet configured
- Drop Invalid HTTP requests
- Enable Selective Acknowledgement
- Configure Window Scaling
- Use TCP tuning for XenApp & XenDesktop
- The management interface on port 80 and enabled on all interfaces
- ACLs not configured
- And my personal favorite finding (twice this year): NSROOT password still set to default. Talk about an easy hack!

We have a lot to cover, so let's dive in!

Layers	• **Access**
Success Lanes	• Design • Build
Prerequisites	• NetScaler (Citrix ADC) • Microsoft IIS • SSL and TLS • Citrix StoreFront
Importance	🎸 🎸 🎸 🎸
User Impact	🎸 🎸
Security Impact	🎸 🎸 🎸 🎸 🎸
Difficulty	🎸 🎸 🎸

Change NetScaler Password

Let's start with my favorite. If you are running the default NSROOT password, for the love of all that is holy, change it! If I need to explain why, I'll say that this is only a slightly bigger problem than you putting your username and password on a sticky-note and sticking it to your monitor. Just change the nsroot password and secure it. Please.

For advanced points, many teams tie the administrative consoles with Active Directory accounts. But I'll be honest- if you are still using the default nsroot password, I don't think describing that particular procedure is beneficial for you.

If you aren't, I have two bits of advice:

1. If you do change the NSROOT password (which is a good idea on occasion) be sure it isn't used by any monitoring tools or other outside uses.

2. Enabling LDAP (ie Active Directory) authentication is a great way to not have to maintain passwords on the device. Here's how to make it happen: Citrix Article CTX123782 [https://ctxpro.com/CHlinks/#16]. All I ask is that you take the time to design this well before implementing it! I have seen a lot of mistakes and frustration with this process. Reach out to the Citrix Hero community if you need help!

NetScaler Firmware Vulnerable to Attack

CVE-2017-14602

On September 25th, 2017 Citrix suddenly pulled the firmware releases of nearly every NetScaler version from their website. The problem was a very serious flaw (CVE-2017-14602) in older firmware version going back clear to 10.1 that would allow an attacker to bypass the normal security and gain direct access to the administrative interface. Needless to say, it got a lot of people's attention... but not enough. In 2019 I was STILL finding vulnerable firmware even in enterprise-level deployments that I examined in 2018. The worst part is that there have been additional vulnerabilities since then and the story is the same:

In nearly every case the result was the same: The firmware in use was the same as the original deployment or downloaded version. There had never been an update.

The first part of the fix is easy enough- upgrade your firmware. The second part involves changing your ACLs, which we'll talk about in the advanced section. I find this to be optimal... but optional.

CVE-2019-19781

Well, since it's now March 2020 as I'm writing this I may as well include the single largest ADC event I have ever encountered. The need for keeping up to date on security releases related to Firmware or default settings became very apparent in December of 2019 as a flaw in literally every Citrix ADC and many other websites worldwide were exposed and potentially very easily compromised. While Citrix moved relatively quickly to provide a workaround and later a patch – unfortunately the flaw involved every exposed Citrix Gateway and was easily scanned for over port 443. When crackers learned they could mine cryptocurrency as part of the flaw – the Internet itself quite literally exploded with traffic attempting to find and exploit unpatched gateways. The bigger problem was that people either didn't get notices or when they did, they figured it was like every other patch that they would wait for the next firmware release.

Big mistake. The nature of the flaw turned ugly as people realized that all passwords in the nsconfig file could be read, along with the hashes for all SSL certs.

Which means that simple patching was not enough. You had to change passwords, re-key certs and in any case with a compromise, completely reinstall the firmware. Simple firmware update was not enough because the core files in the firmware itself could have been compromised and would not be replaced in the current process.

It was shocking just how many people ignored or put off even my warnings https://ctxpro.com/CHlinks/#17.

I won't go into detail on how to resolve the issue in this book – instead I'll just say that if you run a Citrix Gateway, your Hero moment is being proactive. Citrix has an email list to inform you of updates. Set keyword alerts on Google and Twitter. Stay informed. It is your task to protect your users and company! If you need help getting this done, reach out to us and we'll see about getting someone to help you. Aside from my own consulting work I know a great many other consultants that may have time. But the big Hero lesson? Being proactive is key.

You can learn more from our website at https://ctxpro.com/CHlinks/#18

NetScaler Gateway Not Scoring an A+ at SSLLabs.com

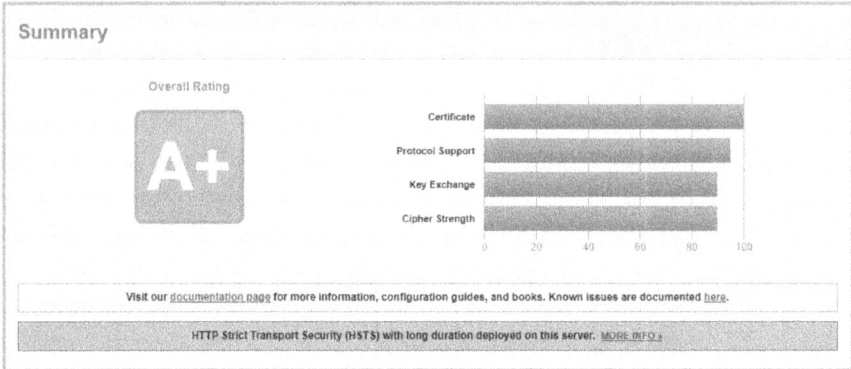

Summary

Overall Rating

A+

Certificate
Protocol Support
Key Exchange
Cipher Strength

Visit our documentation page for more information, configuration guides, and books. Known issues are documented here.

HTTP Strict Transport Security (HSTS) with long duration deployed on this server. MORE INFO »

Figure 2: The Coveted A+ Score at SSL Labs

I had written about this a few times in 2016 [https://ctxpro.com/CHlinks/#19] and again in 2017 [https://ctxpro.com/CHlinks/#20].

Essentially, if you have an external-facing SSL virtual server (NetScaler Gateway or otherwise) you will want to strive for an A+ score to make sure your attack surface is lowered externally. Fortunately, even following the 2016 instructions will still net you a good score and my testing in 2019 has still shown customers using the 2017 advice are still getting A scores. Citrix published an article in 2018 [https://ctxpro.com/CHlinks/#21] as well that is worth the read.

However, with the adoption of TLS 1.3 and a few other updates, expect some scoring changes coming up soon, but you know what I'm already seeing out there?

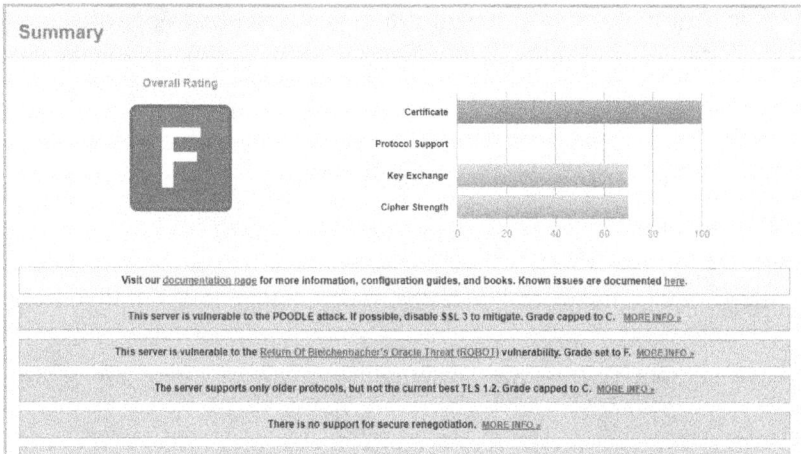

Figure 3: If you see this- time to either fix it or hire someone who can.

That's right. 7 of 10 of the sites I observed in 2018 were still vulnerable in a way that was visible to the world (the SSLLabs test is done externally on what the world sees). In several of these cases, the F was from the firmware problem I mentioned above.

This is a massive topic but is also very frequently updated. Please do start with a visit to the links above to get full details! Here's what you'll need:

- Perform an analysis at SSLLabs.com and look at the score you are getting and why.

- Keep an eye out for very bad things like still using SSL2 or 3, really old Cipher Suites and vulnerabilities like BEAST, POODLE, and others. The ideal Cipher suite combinations are an interesting discussion and it honestly depends on both your version of NetScaler and what your endpoint devices will support. The good news is that the latest NetScaler firmware builds support a secure profile that takes care of this for you!

- Make sure your SSL server is not vulnerable to ROBOT. If you upgraded to firmware above the ones I listed previously you should be fine.

- If your endpoint devices will support it, remove support for SSL3, TLS1 and TLS 1.1 (this is crucial to test and have a support statement around)

- Check the detection of Secure Renegotiation and Forward Secrecy (PFS). Those settings may indicate a need to adjust your TCP settings on the NetScaler as I recommend.
- Always run an analysis of the NetScaler's support file at the Citrix CIS website (https://cis.citrix.com) to look for other problem spots.
- Disable Client and server side SSL Renegotiation CTX123680 and enable HSTS CTX224172 if possible [https://ctxpro.com/CHlinks/#22].

Which is all great. But the day I originally wrote this I found a new rating:

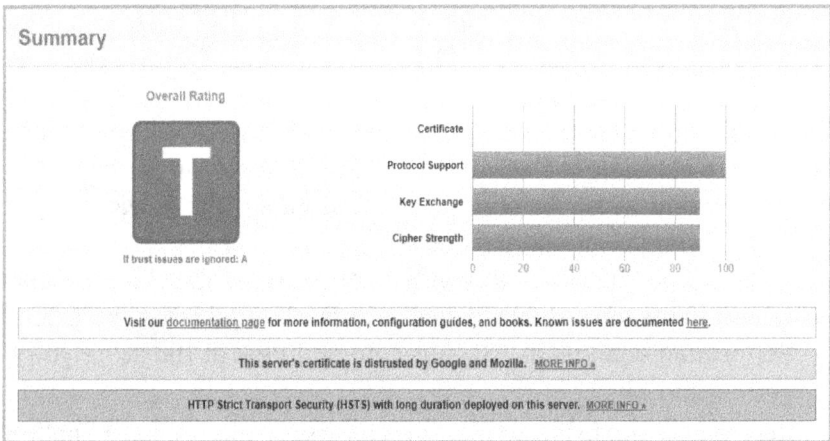

Figure 4: The T Rating

Why? If you are using a certificate that can't be trusted by Google (typically a Symantec certificate of a certain generation according to a Qualys article [https://ctxpro.com/CHlinks/#23] you may, forgive the pun, have Trust Issues.

If you want a worse pun – a customer of mine said that "T" stood for "Time for a new root cert"

SSL Performance and Security

An additional word about SSL Ciphers. The security element of cipher sets is largely talked about the most. However, a key you should know is that performance is also essential. Specifically, performance in the case of what I'm talking about – the ICA protocol.

In other words, ciphers for general web traffic may be different from a performance perspective than those for NetScaler Gateway. Be sure when researching that you take those into consideration. And honestly- I don't want to muddy the water with detail about the way these things work.

That would be yet another book! That, and it changes rapidly. What you should do is get in the habit of checking the Citrix documentation for the particular firmware version you have. I will say if you're interested in learning more, looking more into ECDSA ciphers may be a useful topic for you. Not to mention learning more about DTLS and the proper cipher support for that functionality. If you support teams overseas, for example- you really should learn more about DTLS because that is what allows UDP based protocols like EDT to work over SSL.

For now, my suggestion is to keep it simple until you know for a fact all endpoints will support the advanced ciphers. Fortunately, the SSLabs testing tool will show you how the ciphers configured for the tested URL are performing. Even a slightly better cipher group is better than the usual defaults. Again, defaults are meant to be there to support the widest range of devices and configurations, not to protect you.

Leading Practice Configuration

Just as in Chapter 1- the defaults for the NetScaler are meant for initial deployment. Once you have deployed, the idea is that you'd lock the device down. This is easy to miss, and would explain why over 90% of customers I've assessed over the last 3 years have missed it. But not you, #CitrixHero! You can find more information about these settings at CTX121149 [https://ctxpro.com/CHlinks/#24], but this is crucial: TEST and be aware of your settings. While enabling Nagle's Algorithm and Enabling Selective Acknowledgement are beneficial and rarely have effects, settings such as Window Scaling and dropping invalid HTTP packets may need further examination based on your networking setup. 9 times out of 10 however, I find that all the recommended settings make sense.

LDAP And Domain Password Security

During the crisis in 2019-2020 I found a new bad practice. See if this sounds familiar or likely:

During the installation of the NetScaler/Citrix Gateway, an LDAP account and password is needed for authentication so that users can log on. Many people got in a hurry or made assumptions. I will confess that I have also quite often made assumptions in this area. The assumption? What permissions or groups to which the LDAP account belongs. I've learned to double-check at this point!

In January 2020 I found that 3 out of every 5 ADCs I evaluated were using LDAP accounts with some kind of elevated group membership. 2 of every 5 were using domain admin accounts.

When the late 2019 flaw was exposed, one of the areas of potential compromise was the password to these LDAP accounts. While fortunately not every single one in my case was compromised – the point is that you never know.

Here's some points to consider:
- Multi-Factor Authentication doesn't protect you here. If the Gateway (or VPN, or whatever) is compromised they could set up a backdoor or authentication method that doesn't require MFA.
- The LDAP Account for ADC does NOT need to have any elevation, and should just be a standard domain user only. The account should have no group memberships other than those used to restrict interactive logons with said account.
- If your ADC is ever compromised, it is CRUCIAL that you change every password on your network as a precaution. Yes, every single one. It may be scary to communicate something like that to management, but better to say something now than after a massive compromise gets traced back to your department.
- Rotate LDAP accounts and passwords on a regular basis

Lock Down Management Interfaces
Again, the default setting for NetScaler is to allow for setup to occur cleanly with the assumption it will be locked down. So, a lot of people miss that they have management functionality on interfaces where this is not intended. Disable Enable Management Access control, Telnet, SSH, and GUI on all Non-Management IPs. More information here about restricting NSIPs to only allow management applications: CTX126736

Also see the "Enable Secure Access to NetScaler GUI" CTX111531. Access both at https://ctxpro.com/CHlinks/#25.

Optional – Define Interface ACLs

One of the best ways to defend against future attacks is to lock down the administrative (management) interfaces so that only specific IPs are allowed. We call this defining Access Control Lists (ACLs). Be careful with this setting. See my 2017 article for more details about how to design for this, but you can set IPs or a range of IPs as trusted utility servers or PCs to allow access to the admin functions. Everything else is blocked, including internal requests, making it very secure. Note- you'll need to do this on all NetScalers as this setting does not get copied via HA.

Other Access Layer Issues

StoreFront Using Plaintext

This issue affects two different areas. The first is more obvious; when you have a NetScaler Gateway (Citrix Gateway) you are using port 443. Great! But what I am finding in assessments is that the StoreFront connection to the NetScaler is still using port 80 (Plaintext HTML). This makes this communication susceptible to Man in the Middle attacks [see https://ctxpro.com/CHlinks/#26] where information can be intercepted mid-stream but still passed along. The problem here is personally identifiable information including passwords can pass along this path. While it is a little more work to create SSL to the internal StoreFront servers but if you are using them, secure them at all points!

Bonus: XML Service Using Plaintext

The second way that StoreFront uses plaintext is, believe it or not, worse. The XML services that are used on controllers are an aging, yet still viable method by which the StoreFront sends information to the Controller regarding the user. The XML service communicates back to the StoreFront server as to which icons to load, *and a token to login to a server*. So, if intercepted... well, you get the point. Fortunately, this is rare and would only really occur in an inside attack, but my notion is to always treat endpoint devices as potential threats and secure the network as much as possible!

In older days you typically had IIS installed to your Controllers- if you do the instructions to secure this traffic are at CTX200415.

But if you do not have IIS installed (in an ideal world, you wouldn't), you will probably want to examine my article on the topic as well [https://ctxpro.com/CHlinks/#27].

To give a general idea, your goal is to bind a certificate using a command line for each controller, but make sure to use a certificate that can be either loaded or trusted by the StoreFront servers.

As you can imagine, there are dozens more things I typically recommend on these topics- and I don't even consider myself an authority on NetScaler. However, keep an eye out on ctxpro.com. If you, for some reason, aren't subscribed to the newsletter, you really should be. When there are important updates, we will typically notify the list.

Chapter 3: Workload Placement and Sizing

A company had hired us to evaluate why their system seemed to randomly slow down, even though they had recently doubled their host servers. We (of course) made several recommendations for tuning, however one they consistently ignored because their VMware representative was advising them that it was not required. Read that again: we were hired as experts but they were listening to someone with no context.

What was the point of contention here?

They had all VMs in a single cluster.

Eventually, they listened and separated the clusters – one for the infrastructure and another for their XenDesktop resource VMs. When we followed up with them, we found a very happy CIO. User complaints had vanished, but they also had a predictable way to scale – knowing how many users could be serviced within a single host server.

But like any hero, a #CitrixHero sometimes has to fight for what is right.

Layers	• **Cloud**
Success Lanes	• Design • Build
Prerequisites	• Hypervisor • BIOS and Physical Hardware
Importance	🎸 🎸 🎸 🎸 🎸
User Impact	🎸 🎸 🎸 🎸
Security Impact	🎸
Difficulty	🎸 🎸

Workload Placement

Okay, great, you've tuned the OS of the VMs and your access layer. But for around 60% of the companies I assessed last year, another big problem was robbing them of value: not paying attention to the unique requirements and tunings for Citrix Virtual Apps within their physical server (hypervisor) setups. While this can often become an almost religious debate- I stand behind these recommendations, having seen improvements in dozens of environments since 2010 when I started drawing a hard line on doing things this way. You can debate with whitepapers all day, but the bottom line is that I've seen this work even when it seems to make no sense. Sometimes you must swallow your pride and trust, and that's what I'm asking a lot of you with doubts to do now. Trust over 100 other experts that have seen the same results along with myself. Hypervisor tuning matters. Of course, you may have a bit of a hard time convincing some teams that manage the hypervisor and are still getting poor information. Unfortunately, I see that all the time.

What I'm seeing emerge once again these days is an old practice which I thought for sure we had done away with: All the VMs in a single cluster and let the Hypervisor sort them out. This presents a... host... of problems (the puns will continue until Leading Practices are followed, folks):

1) You are no longer able to predict how much adding new users will cost in terms of hardware.
2) You cannot accurately predict how many Server VDA VMs you will need.
3) You cannot predictably assure performance from one user to the next due to other workloads that cohabitate the same host. For example, when a SQL server goes into freakout mode on the same CPU as your Server VDAs- you'll have users complaining even though CPU is not showing any signs of the issue.
4) Different workloads can tolerate different overcommit ratios. With a mixed workload style, you may have your user workloads on hosts that are actually overcommitted.

I am sure that even as people were reading my statement above tension started to show up. Doubts. But the reality is that user-based workloads behave very differently than the average hypervisor administrator realizes. An RDSH server (XenApp) with 30 users is going to behave very differently than a SQL or Exchange server. Therefore, placing them on the same host means you are making the hypervisor essentially pick favorites. But placing the same kind of workloads on a physical host has a kind of magic, reducing the conflicts and, more importantly, making the scale predictable. We'll talk more about how many VMs and their configuration later- a very important aspect to avoid oversubscription. But to do that properly, we first need to make sure that our Resources will always have the right backing and no conflicts. This can't be done without isolation.

The solution to this first problem is to isolate your user workloads from the backend servers completely. This is typically done by dedicating Resource clusters for Server VDAs and Desktop VDAs with all Control components located in the main infrastructure cluster. This has the benefit of allowing you to use a different licensing, version, or even type of hypervisor for your resources, which typically do not need things like HA and backups. The hypervisor requirements are different than the other production clusters. Further, if your team has skillsets of supporting multiple hypervisor types, but you primarily use VMware, you may even want to consider a high-performing but simplified hypervisor solution for the Resource hosts such as XenServer (Citrix Hypervisor) or Nutanix Acropolis. However- I do NOT recommend learning a new hypervisor just for this purpose. If your team only knows one hypervisor well, keep the same for your Resource cluster.

If you don't have a lot of hosts available or are concerned about keeping N+1 for two clusters rather than one, the second method is to use Host DRS (or its equivalent). This will place the workloads to preferred hosts when they boot. In most cases, you would have two Host DRS groups- Control and Resource. In the event of a failure, you will still be able to load VMs onto the other hosts temporarily, but only when capacity is exceeded. I'm encountering this option a lot in smaller and mid-sized environments, but I never recommend this if you have more than 6 hosts. At that point, you're usually better off isolating workloads completely. You should also keep in mind that this method may require some 'babysitting' during maintenance to be sure workloads end up back on their intended hosts.

Workload Sizing

Now to sizing. This is the other area I see massive amounts of *fail* lately. Someone read a whitepaper that said to configure their XenApp servers with 4 vCPU and 8 GB RAM… and wonder why they can only get 15 users before it starts slowing down. The reality here is that you need to default to scaling UP with your users per VM until you reach a performance threshold and then scale OUT with more servers. The way to do this is to increase the resources per VM – CPU, Memory, and Storage. So how do you know how much you can use? This is an 'it depends' answer if there ever was one. But once again, this is why we isolate workloads. We need to know how many CPU cores and RAM we have comfortably available (N+1 or N+2 is typically the threshold here).

For example, say we have hosts with two 14-core CPUs and 256 GB RAM. To be safe, we declare that about 200 GB RAM is our safely available amount, to give the hypervisor some room and some 'just in case' room. We also ALWAYS want our user workloads, be it Desktop or Server OS, to fully reserve the RAM in the hypervisor. This prevents the usage of a paging disk (required in VMware if you don't use this option, sucking down storage space) and is another reason to isolate the workloads. We'll use Server OS for our workload examples. Some feasible options in terms of memory (you can use any memory value you want in Windows these days) are:

- 6 VMs at 32 GB
- 4 VMs at 48 GB
- 12 VMs at 16 GB

Next, we turn to CPU. Here's where it gets interesting. An often-overlooked bit of math that you must do to be successful in terms of Citrix is division. I won't go into the full explanation of NUMA vs UMA, but in a nutshell, you want your workloads to cohabitate the same physical CPU as much as possible. This prevents the need for crossing memory bus lanes and a host of other implications that can slow down the hypervisor itself.

We do this by setting our VMs to a value that matches the CPU's NUMA values. You should always confirm these, but they are typically divisible numbers of the physical (not virtual) cores. I will tell you that I chose the 14 core processor for a very good reason- it only has 4 valid vCPU NUMA values: 1, 2, 7 and 14. While you *can* use less- research has shown that for

Server OS especially, you are better off having fewer VMs with more CPUs than you are with more VMs with smaller CPUs because of the way the hypervisor essentially is forced to arrange workloads on the CPUs.

So in our case, we know that we are best served by configuring our VMs with 7 vCPUs – so because this will be a much larger VM, we are looking at either 32 or 48 GB RAM. To determine the right sizing, we need to know our tolerable CPU Overcommit ratio. In most cases, I have observed, 1.2:1 is about right for Server OS, whereas Desktop OS can often scale to 5:1 or up to 12:1 in some cases I have seen. Again- 'it depends'. For us, we know that 1.2x28 (the total of physical CPU cores on the machine) is 33.6. Dividing by 7 gives us 4.8, which we safely round DOWN to 4.

So- your CPU Blade should have FOUR VMs with 7 vCPU and 48 GB RAM.

BUT... how many users per VM?

This is another common Citrix mistake! We shouldn't care about users per VM anywhere near as much as we need to determine how many users per PHYSICAL BLADE/HOST.

Think of it this way. If I was to put a pair of virtual machines on your laptop- how many users do you think would safely be able to use it before it became, well, unusable? Even if these are VMs intended for many or few users, the physical hardware can only do so much. The hypervisor doesn't magically fix this. Any host will have limits that must be anticipated and respected. So now that you've isolated your workloads- good news! You can figure out those numbers easily by simple division- Number of users per host divided by the number of VMs. Now, keep in mind that mileage may vary here based on the applications and Operating system... however, there is one mistake that you should NOT make:

If Per-VM performance is bad because of the amount of users, you need to adjust the number of HOSTS, not the number of VMs. Adding VMs to a physical host will degrade performance for all users because the physical limitations have not changed.

The Rule of 5 and 10

Here's the thing. Unless you have the tools, time, and patience to figure out EXACTLY how many users to have per blade- you need a simple rule to start with, then further optimize from there.

"More what you'd call guidelines than actual rules…"

-Hector Barbosa (Pirates of the Caribbean)

Thanks here go to Citrix Consulting and especially Nick Rintalan for figuring the math out on this one. As a matter of fact, he and I worked together for a while, trying to figure out a very overly complicated spreadsheet to try and calculate this. I was delighted when he noticed the way the numbers always seemed to work out and declare the "Rule of 5 and 10". I could go into the underlying arithmetic here, but let's keep it simple. You can determine how many users can be on a host, based on the *physical* CPU cores (not the threads (virtual), but physical cores).

- Desktop OS workloads: 5 users per pCPU core
- Server OS workloads: 10 users per pCPU core

So again in our example, blades with two 14-core processors (28 pCores) we can expect 280 Server OS users or 140 VDI users. Note, this is *active* users, not VMs. In our example, it means we should expect a maximum of 70 users per VM. While this is possible- it may not always be practical. Load testing is essential to determine the exact number. Now that we know the hardware can handle it, we end up in the domain of the OS itself. Typically I have seen an appropriately sized and tuned Server 2012 R2 VM safely handle easily 120 users running fairly light apps, but when using a published desktop, the numbers dropped to about 50 users per VM max. Sometimes, you may need to add an additional VM- keep to the NUMA values and try not to exceed the overcommit ratio and you'll usually be fine. Test, Test, Test!

So if we have 3000 users, we know we need 11 host servers (+1 for redundancy = 12). And, as an added #CitrixHero moment, when the VP of IT asks you how much it will cost to add another 500 users… you'll be able to give them a REAL answer! Scalability is fun!

Reference https://ctxpro.com/CHlinks/#28.

The question you're likely asking yourself is, does this work in the real world? Yes. Yes, it does. I can point to countless examples that I won't get into here. But my friend Steve took my advice and it worked pretty well for him.

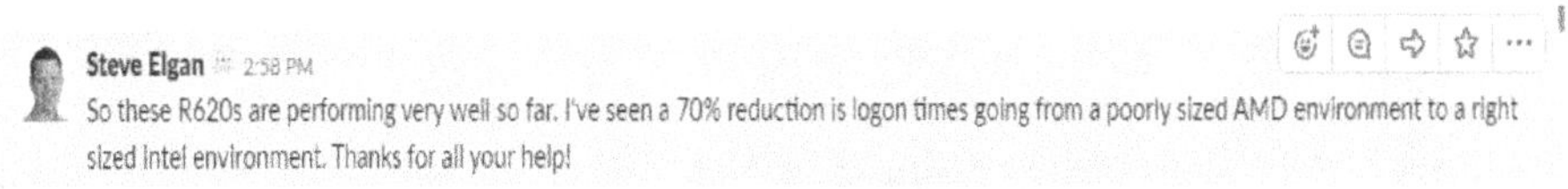

Steve Elgan 2:58 PM
So these R620s are performing very well so far. I've seen a 70% reduction is logon times going from a poorly sized AMD environment to a right sized Intel environment. Thanks for all your help!

Figure 5: A Thank you note from CTA Steve Elgan

Hardware Virtualization Settings

Several times in 2018 and 2019 I was surprised to find that the underlying BIOS settings for physical hosts were not set correctly. Depending on the setting, this can be a MASSIVE problem, so while it isn't common… I thought I'd include this because of its additional impact.

If you find your VMs are slow and running 100% much of the time, check your BIOS settings. Even if things are running fine - *check your BIOS settings anyway*. You may find that C-States are enabled. This seems like a great idea until you put a Hypervisor on top of it. Remember, servers typically ship for compatibility and to meet power usage standards by default. You have to tune them once you get them! (sensing a theme here?)

Common Mistakes (not just Citrix, but any Hypervisor):

- C-States enabled (this allows the CPU to throttle and changes the CPU percentage calculation)
- Virtualization not enabled (breaks the hypervisor's ability to function as, well, a hypervisor)
- Hyperthreading not enabled (yes, the rule of 5 and 10 assumed HT is on)
- Power settings not set properly (typically should be the "Power" or "no power management" setting)
- Also very much related to the NUMA settings above, make sure to check for the correct QPI 'snoop' modes and don't always trust the 'auto' setting to give you Cluster On-Die (CoD). For example, failure to do this on a 14 core processor can be problematic. This processor tends to array the silicon in a 6+8 configuration and uses CoD to present the proper NUMA values. Without it, performance can suffer.

45

Power Management Matters

An article that is worth reviewing is from Jasper Geelen (LoginVSI): https://ctxpro.com/CHlinks/#29

Jasper notes that power management settings specifically are different per vendor, as are the names used, but almost all allow options to either let the OS handle power or various other settings. While you can let your hypervisor control these settings, you should know that it isn't typically dynamic. My recommendation is to manually lock the BIOS in its highest power state for any VDI or RDSH workloads. In some cases, this means turning power management off completely. How this is phrased depends on your vendor.

> *"Faulty power management is the most common but easiest to fix VDI mistake. Configuring this properly can save your users a lot of energy (and) user experience will increase"*
>
> *Mark Plettenberg, LoginVSI and fellow Citrix CTA*

LoginVSI found that this can be a difference of 64% of performance. Go ahead and read that again, I'll wait.
This means that in a great many cases, more than half of the available performance the machines expect… simply isn't there. This data holds up in the real world, in my case even *better* than the synthetic testing showed.

My favorite case of this was one of those times when an assessment being performed paid for itself three times over, simply because we caught this one thing that an engineer had made the assumption was correct. Their servers had C states enabled, and it was seriously affecting their scalability. The client was able to cancel an order for over $45,000 because upon enabling the power management correction, their problems with VMs reporting 100% CPU went away. They were immediately able to more than double the number of users on each blade and still had better performance than previously there. When combined with other tuning suggestions, they estimate that they will be able to go another three years without additional purchases. So, it seems simple enough, but one miss or assumption can literally cost that much.

What if you could save your company $20,000 consulting bill by simply double-checking these settings? I'll say it again – be the Citrix Hero! Or- you know, don't do it and call me. I'll take the money.

Additional Reading

My friend Helge Klein wrote about this in 2013 (see https://ctxpro.com/CHlinks/#30) using HP servers as an example. If you have a Cisco UCS system, I suggest having a look at their article, paying particular attention to Table 4. [https://ctxpro.com/CHlinks/#31]

Chapter 4: Provisioning Services Tuning

"We've invested thousands in fast storage. Why aren't we getting the performance we were promised?"

I sat across the conference room table, also wondering why others with less capable hardware were getting much better performance.

You can probably imagine the look on the person's face a few days later when I delivered the report stating that they did not need expensive hardware solutions to deliver world-class speed from Provisioning Server workloads. The solution had existed within Windows since Server 2008 R2.

All they needed was a little more RAM. They had squandered thousands on a VXRail system they didn't need. Ouch.

The good news for you is that with a little proactive monitoring and smart math, you can get industry-leading results as well… without expensive storage systems.

Layers	• **Resource**
	• **Control**
Success Lanes	• Design
	• Build
	• Understand
Prerequisites	• Windows Desktop & Server OS Knowledge
	• Image Deployment Design
	• PVS & MCS Fundamentals
Importance	🎸 🎸 🎸
User Impact	🎸 🎸 🎸
Security Impact	🎸
Difficulty	🎸 🎸

PVS Target Device Performance

Before we get to the Provisioning Services (PVS) Server issue I noted in the introduction (anticipation killing you? Good. It'll make you pay attention!) I wanted to first get a little more into how PVS works and help you understand why Memory is the most essential aspect of this network-based protocol. Yeah. Memory. Not Network speed. Not Hard Drive speed or SAN speed. Memory.

Problem #1 - Summary VDA Performance Lags

Problem Description

User experience suffers, especially later in the day. System pauses are experienced without subsequent CPU utilization spikes. While OS Optimization helps, the overall user experience seems to suffer regardless of how many programs are open. Workspace Environment Manager has helped memory and CPU issues but not solved the issue.

Troubleshooting Notes

The Administrators note that the problems do seem to increase with additional sessions being active but cannot explain when the same amount of sessions at an earlier point in the day are not experiencing the slowdowns, so they suspect that the number of sessions may not be the primary factor.

Storage Engineers are concerned as IOPS do increase toward the end of the day but are still way below what the system is rated to perform. A recent move to an all-flash array has not had a noticeable impact so they have encouraged looking more at the programs themselves or that it is a 'Citrix problem'. Network Engineers report no issues or notable differences between the beginning and end of the workday.

EXERCISE:

WORK WITH YOUR STORAGE TEAM TO FIND OUT HOW MANY IOPS YOUR CVAD VMS HAVE BEEN CONSUMING.

IF POSSIBLE, DENOTE HOW MANY TIMES THE VMS EXPERIENCE WAIT TIMES TO READ OR WRITE FROM DISK.

Background: How the Target Device Works

While I'd love to do a deep dive of how PVS works in detail in this chapter, suffice it to say (at least the best way I've heard it explained to me) that

PVS creates a read-only UDP-based virtual iSCSI stream which allows multiple target devices to boot from and simulate Hard Disk reads from this stream. Thousands of target VMs can be serviced from a single image (which is what makes PVS so attractive). But it is read-only in this mode, meaning that it can't be corrupted and is inherently consistent. Further, high availability is assured because if the target device does not get a response from the host, it can automatically switch to another initiator (server) in real-time. Because your Operating System is used to waiting for data all the time with the hard disk in your machine this is not unusual for it; the target device software 'tricks' it into behaving as if it has a hard disk. The amazing thing about how it does this is by only streaming the data that is requested! Contrary to what you may think- the entire disk image is NOT streamed at once. Only those sectors requested to read are streamed (keep the 'sectors' aspect of this in mind- this is a block device stream, NOT a data stream like SMB or NFS). The advantage is that, again, there is a shockingly low amount of data transmitted all at once. However, there are two primary problem areas in this scenario:

1) What happens to data that changes as the target OS is running?
2) What happens when the target OS has to wait for read data?

To understand the first problem, think of … well, any computing device. Regardless of your PC, laptop, phone… maybe even your watch. There are two key functions involved when it comes to data. Read and Write. As we mentioned above, reads are happening across the network in normal operations. Writes are where it gets really interesting for PVS. After all, once the Operating System writes data from memory to the storage it expects it to be there. If it cannot write, it generally will not work. The Target Device Software (which by the way can now be Windows Desktop or Server OS as well as Linux workloads) then must solve the problem of where to store the data since it cannot write to the boot 'disk'. It does this by using a temporary storage system which is writable that contains the modified blocks. When the OS requests data from that block, the Target Device software keeps it's own FAT table in memory (I'm simplifying how this works here, remember, this isn't a deep dive per se) and knows when the request is from a modified block or a block that needs to be streamed from the server. So where is the data that persists for the session live?

Changed data blocks during a target device's lifecycle is referred to as Disk Deltas. The amount of data this represents depends on the fragmentation of data on the source disk and the block size. A 1 KB delta on a 64 KB block would still be a 64 KB disk delta.

With PVS there are a few primary ways this data can be stored. However, what is true of ALL of these is that it must be temporary storage. Remember, this is not storing the formatted data. It is storing the modified BLOCKS. This means that having the data persist really is neither practical nor in some cases really even possible. Nonetheless, there can be hundreds of thousands of modifications that occur during the powered-on cycle of the VM (often referred to as a lifecycle in this case). While there have been several methods to store the data over the years, a few stand out as primary.

- **Cache in Server RAM** – the modified blocks are stored in a virtual RAM allocation on the server, essentially as a virtual Microsoft RAM Disk (VHD). Read here that once the server runs out of RAM, everything dies, making this a pretty unattractive option. VHD was a great format but was not without issues in that data is not always 'trimmed' when deleted. Meaning the longer your machine is booted, the more deltas are piling up in RAM. I often threatened anyone using this option outside of development that I'd slap them right across the face. It really isn't scalable or practical for production use.

- **Cache on Server Hard Disk** – this was the old default, and this functionality is still used temporarily by the XenDesktop Setup Wizard when machines are being created. Data is stored on the specified cache location for the Store as a single flat file specific to that target device. The advantage is that you don't have to worry about local storage for your VM. The disadvantages are managing said data at the PVS server can mean a lot of bloat if you are using local vDisk stores and as we'll talk about soon- it can kill your server's ability to utilize RAM for performance. Still, in some cases like those requiring strict PCI compliance, it sometimes made sense.

- **Cache in Device RAM** – Changed blocks are stored directly in the device's RAM. This performed really well, however just as with Server RAM, once it's gone, it's gone and the device blue screens. How confident are you in how many disk deltas you will have?
- **Cache on Device Hard Disk** – the go-to option for nearly a decade, a virtual (or if physical, just a hard drive) is attached to the Target Device and a system file is added to the disk containing changed blocks just as with Cache on Server Hard Disk.
- **Cache in Device RAM with Failover to Hard Disk** – This is the single most exciting development in PVS since Versioning. This option not only puts a RAM cache in front of the Cache to Device Hard Disk style option but supercharged it in two key ways:
  - A more advanced virtual hard disk structure (vhdx) is more efficient and supports TRIM to reduce blocks used.
  - Data is only written to the disk when the RAM is exceeded (and only when this occurs, drastically reducing the disk IO).

I know, I know… I said this wasn't going to be a deep dive. Consider this bonus information, Citrix Hero!

Solving the Performance Issue

The first thing I want you to consider is that if you are not using Cache in Device RAM with Failover to Hard Disk then in almost every case this is what you need to change first. In terms of performance, stability, and usability it is my go-to for 99% of cases. I'd say 100%, but that's just risky, even though since 2016 I have insisted on it 100% of the time. The two keys are the way RAM is utilized and the new structure's ability to TRIM data blocks that have been deleted. Remember what I said earlier about deltas being blocks, not data? In cases like Outlook, Internet Explorer, Chrome, and more, there are thousands of bits of data that are written and then deleted over the lifecycle of the user session. My research into this, often indicated that a shocking amount of IO is DELETE operations. Now, remember what I said about the nature of blocks and that the cache blocks, not data. So you have a 1000 temporary files, each let's say 1k each or less. That would mean you'd need to write and delete 1 GB of data, right? Wrong. If the modified blocks are fragmented, you could be writing between 1 and 64 GB of blocks, depending on the allocation and layout.

AT LAST, we've come to my first key recommendation!

Cache in RAM sizing should strive to store as many Delta SECTORS as required for your use case.

I say *strive* for a very good reason. Getting this exact is near impossible. But *even a cache that is too small will still reduce overall disk write IO for your target devices*! This is because data is always written first to the RAM cache, then to the disk. This means the OS is not waiting for confirmation of the write. As far as it's concerned, the business is finished. The impact on performance is more significant than you may think.

Many issues of apparent slowness on a Resource VM are often the OS waiting for read and write confirmation, not slowness of CPU. Use Performance Monitor to keep an eye on disk wait times.

I'll say right away that even with data to the contrary, Citrix still chose to issue a warning if you exceed about 64 MB of Cache in RAM. My research and experience tell me that you should START with the following values (more on fine-tuning soon):

OS Type	Session Length	Workload	RAM Cache to Start
Desktop	Under 2 hrs	Simple apps (no SaaS)	64 MB
Desktop	Over 2 hrs	Simple apps (no SaaS)	128 MB
Desktop	Under 2 hrs	Task Work + Internet	256 MB
Desktop	Over 2 hrs	Task Work + Internet	368 MB – 512 MB

OS Type	Session Length	Workload	RAM Cache to Start
Server	Under 2 hrs	Published App (not browsers) – 1 to 30 users	1024 MB (add about 368 MB per 10 users)
Server	Under 2 hrs	Published App (including browsers) – 1 to 20 users	2048 MB (add about 512 MB per 10 users)
Server	All Day	Published App (not browsers) – 1 to 30 users	2048 MB (add about 512 MB per 10 users)
Server	All Day	Published App (including browsers) – 1 to 20 users	4098 MB (monitor and anticipate up to 64 MB additional per user)
Server	Any	Published Desktop	4098 MB per about 20 users active

As you can see, though Server does tend to need more RAM, it also makes much more efficient use of the TRIM capability, especially once the user logs off and the OS 'deletes' the profile and temp data from what it thinks is the disk.

Information Gathering

How do we determine when the OS is 'happy' in this regard? Fortunately, in the case we have here, writes to an attached disk are still recorded in Windows Performance Manager metrics.

Monitor PHYSICAL disk writes to the cache disk device to determine how much write IO is happening. This will let you know if you need to increase or decrease the Cache in RAM value.

EXERCISE:

SET UP A CUSTOM PERFORMANCE MONITOR TO WATCH FOR WHEN THERE ARE A LOT OF
WRITES AND COMPARE TO THE WRITES GOING TO THE PHYSICAL DISK. CHOOSE
A CONSISTENT MONITORING PERIOD (THIS MAY BE MORE DIFFICULT FOR
DESKTOP OS AS THE SESSION MAY EXPIRE).
WRITE THE REPORT TO THE PERSISTENT DISK (NOT TO THE SYSTEM DEFAULT).
EACH DAY OF TESTING, INCREASE THE CACHE IN RAM VALUE OF THE VDISK AND THE
RAM OF THE VM UNTIL THE DISK IO REDUCES. NOTE THAT THERE ARE
ACTUALLY TWO VALUES TO KEEP AN EYE ON- ONE IS THE OVERALL DATA WRITES
(NUMBER OF TIMES WRITES OCCUR) AND THE ACTUAL AMOUNT OF DATA
WRITTEN. DEPENDING ON THE NATURE OF THE DATA THIS WILL MODIFY YOUR
STRATEGY. GENERALLY SPEAKING, THE NUMBER OF WRITES IS WHAT AFFECTS
PERFORMANCE, NOT THE AMOUNT OF DATA WRITTEN.

Resolution

The good news here is that you don't have to modify the VM to change the cache value. That is configured as part of the vDisk properties on the server. However, the bad news is that you will likely need to increase the RAM of each of your target devices to accommodate the design change. If you have several hundred, this can be time-consuming. If you didn't believe me in other lessons, maybe you do now. TEST, VALIDATE, and PERFORM USER ACCEPTANCE TESTING FULLY BEFORE YOU DEPLOY! Do this by creating a UAT group (about 10% of the population) and validating with them performing their regular workday tasks that your values are well-tuned. Remember, you will never get it perfect, and achieving absolute-zero IOPS is nearly impossible. You'll still want data like page file and event logs to be stored directly to the cache (persistent) drive (remember what I said about blocks earlier? Leading Practice is to set up the page file on the disk directly, so you aren't dealing with the block delta issue. A topic for another session, but you can usually increase RAM to decrease page file usage. Fortunately, the PVS target device software is smart enough to compensate for some oversights here, but I always tell people not to push their luck and plan ahead. The page file works in a very similar way to the PVS cache, so there's also really no need or benefit to clearing the page file at the machine shutdown on a PVS target device. Given most virtual hosts have more RAM than they need, I think you'll find you can be slightly aggressive here, and your SAN administrator will thank you. Yes, even with Hyper-Converged storage. Consuming less is always more for everyone else.

Example
(Details changed to protect the innocent)

A customer was ill-informed about the option and feared exceeding 64 MB cache for their server workloads on PVS. Their FibreChannel based LUNs were set up on SSD storage and activating CiRwFtHD had helped. However- the SAN was still quite 'bogged down' with write IO, which was overloading the SAN's caching. SSDs are much faster reading than writing, so many systems will utilize a temporary RAM cache that is flushed as soon as the SSDs are ready to receive the new data. However, if the queue to write data is too large, the RAM Cache still tells the SAN Masthead to wait for writes to be confirmed before continuing to receive new data. Once the threshold is reached, it is pretty much as if the cache wasn't even there. Once this happens, the PVS target software is held to the same restriction, which forces a slowdown. Worse, in this particular case, the wait was not related to the workload being observed, so the staff was very confused as to why users complained.

In cases like this, you may often find that other workloads have been 'snuck' onto the SSD storage or hear claims that the system is 'performance tiered' to move workloads dynamically. The problem is from a storage perspective (as in the bytes written), non-persistent workloads are never the same from day to day, so these kinds of SAN systems can rarely anticipate the performance needed.

By increasing their cache in RAM value to 4098 (4 GB), the overall IOPS dropped below .2 write operation per user per second from the previous 5 per user. With over 5000 users in scope, the reduction increased performance to all but also solved a mysterious problem the Exchange administrators were having with slow searches. In this case – the Exchange data was on a different 'tier' of storage, yet the IOPS from the VDI LUNs were still impacting it! Don't always believe what you hear in regards to how isolated these systems are in terms of performance!

Solutions to Test
This problem tends to be caused because either the Cache In RAM with Failover to Disk feature has not been configured or has not been

configured with adequate RAM. As with any change, test with IT, validate with a smaller population representative of the production workloads prior to deploying at large.

Solution Steps
1. Observe real-world usage using Performance Monitor
2. Increase both the Cache In RAM value and the device RAM until IO reductions are achieved
3. If more granular data is required, look into tools and scripts to monitor the utilization of the write cache

Additional Considerations:
- Defragment the master image prior to deployment – remember, fewer block allocations mean less caching has to occur and fewer block deltas to write!
- Assure Antivirus software does not have scheduled scans for MCS or PVS-provided VDAs
- Properly configure Citrix Optimizer (see Chapter 1)
- Use Citrix Workspace Environment Manager to control CPU and Memory resource priorities and to free up RAM, especially on Server OS VDAs
- Cache sizing is per vDisk, not per catalog as with MCS. This means if you require different cache sizes, unfortunately, you may have to copy/import vDisks. Best to try to go with the highest value required whenever possible.

MCS Considerations
In a very similar fashion, a recent addition for Machine Creation Services (MCS) has the ability to perform similar caching of disk writes. The concepts are more or less the same… but of course, it wouldn't be all that simple, would it?

How MCS works
In brief, MCS works by instructing the Hypervisor to create a clone of a base VM. First, the Hypervisor API replicates the properties of the VM. Next, depending on the storage and hypervisor, a clone or reference is set up with a delta disk and an identity disk. These disks are not visible to the OS.

MCS, when it debuted, did not have any ability beyond the hypervisor/storage to affect IO Performance. However, Citrix introduced a special driver called MCSIO that could create another (again hidden from the OS) disk and write deltas to that device. The cache would not persist between boots just as PVS... however, it was not without its issues.

Issues with MCS Caching

Full disclosure here, MCSIO is generally something you are better having than not having. However, I noted several issues in deploying it in many scenarios that are worth noting.

- MCSIO is decidedly less efficient than PVS in both its RAM caching, TRIM and overall write performance to the disk. I won't bore you with the specifics. Though some improvements were made using the PVS driver for MCS (for most of you this would be true of LTSR 7 1912 but not 7.15) I am not yet seeing the same level of performance. Time will tell!
- MCSIO tends to require a larger cache footprint- in fact Citrix often recommends having at least 100% of the base disk sized for cache. This is not a hard requirement however – but given that this is a thin assigned space it rarely matters. If space allocation is at a premium, consider at least having the amount of free space on your C drive image plus enough for a page file.
- MCSIO will tend to require more RAM to gain the benefits of RAM Caching.
- MCSIO driver is no longer installed by default (in early 2019). Think ahead when deploying your VDA!

Example

Though iterative performance improvements had been achieved at a client utilizing a Dell Compellent storage array, the team was noting that across-the-board performance was still low even after applying 4098 GB RAM to their MCSIO RAM cache value.

By creating a new machine catalog for each test and monitoring MCS-Specific Performance Monitors, we discovered that increasing the RAM Cache value to over 18 GB was needed to reduce load on their Compellent storage across the organization, even though the LUNs were dedicated to

SSDs that were confirmed not in use for anything but the 13 XenApp servers. The theory here is that the overall 'masthead' for the SAN was being overloaded with IO requests that it was forced to queue.

Test	Data		Results
Day 1 - 2 GB Cache (32 GB RAM)	Citrix MCS Storage Driver		Ratios Disk vs Memory Bytes Written- 607 GB/63 GB (**10:1**)
	Cache disk bytes read	590,442,226,173.0325	
	Cache disk bytes written	606,644,238,226.0031	
	Cache disk high usage watermark	17,603,905,331.4374	
	Cache disk reads	657,801.927	
	Cache disk size	128,849,018,880.0000	
	Cache disk Used	16,683,596,605.3292	
	Cache disk writes	712,273.639	
	Cache memory bytes read	2,923,695,589	Total Writes- 712,273 : 2,917,788 (**1:4**)
	Cache memory bytes written	63,377,948,250.2133	
	Cache memory reads	74,368.225	
	Cache memory target size	2,147,483,648	
	Cache memory used	2,283,704,523	
	Cache memory writes	2,917,788.653	
	Storage driver read requests	272,182.583	
	Storage driver write requests	2,934,267.051	
	System disk bytes read	7,437,868,150	
	System disk bytes written	0.000	
	System disk reads	189,358.515	
	System disk writes	0.000	
Day 2 - 2 GB Cache (32 GB RAM)	Citrix MCS Storage Driver		Ratios Disk to Memory Bytes Written – 1,024 GB /74 GB (**14:1**)
	Cache disk bytes read	1,008,121,810,203.5466	
	Cache disk bytes written	1,024,606,909,574.7948	
	Cache disk high usage watermark	18,207,928,076.6714	
	Cache disk reads	1,104,309.532	
	Cache disk Used	17,085,996,957.7504	
	Cache disk writes	1,159,724.211	
	Cache memory bytes read	6,460,809,608	
	Cache memory bytes written	74,702,544,348.9240	
	Cache memory reads	163,680.287	
	Cache memory target size	2,147,483,648	
	Cache memory used	2,764,811,332	Total Writes – 1,159,724 : 4,682,715 (**1:4**)
	Cache memory writes	4,682,715.674	
	Storage driver read requests	316,954.217	
	Storage driver write requests	4,677,179.645	
	System disk bytes read	3,726,602,421	
	System disk bytes written	0.000	
	System disk reads	135,913.514	
	System disk writes	0.000	

Test	Data		Results
Day 3 - 6 GB Cache (38 GB RAM)	Citrix MCS Storage Driver		Ratios Disk to Memory Bytes Written –
	Cache disk bytes read	122,879,209,738.1963	
	Cache disk bytes written	131,595,830,912.0000	131 GB : 77 GB (**2:1**)
	Cache disk high usage watermark	13,788,773,054.6344	
	Cache disk reads	204,289.118	
	Cache disk Used	12,953,803,843.9147	
	Cache disk writes	250,693.836	
	Cache memory bytes read	4,548,013,022	
	Cache memory bytes written	77,204,014,021.9175	
	Cache memory reads	127,439.825	Total Writes –
	Cache memory target size	8,589,934,592	250,693 : 5,106,425 (**1:20**)
	Cache memory used	8,450,500,569	
	Cache memory writes	5,106,425.169	
	Storage driver read requests	290,668.000	
	Storage driver write requests	5,100,968.592	
	System disk bytes read	5,911,250,914	
	System disk bytes written	0.000	
	System disk reads	160,996.570	
	System disk writes	0.000	
Day 4 16 GB Cache (48 GB RAM)	Citrix MCS Storage Driver		Ratios Disk to Memory Bytes Written – .9 GB : 80 GB (**1:88**)!!!!
	Cache disk bytes read	73,109,508.620	
	Cache disk bytes written	991,700,688.265	
	Cache disk high usage watermark	992,166,437.341	
	Cache disk reads	95.840	
	Cache disk Used	991,752,596.595	
	Cache disk writes	3,565.179	
	Cache memory bytes read	3,237,642,625	
	Cache memory bytes written	80,145,601,912.5574	
	Cache memory reads	94,960.270	Total Writes – 3,565 : 2,923,301 (**1:820**)!!!
	Cache memory target size	17,179,869,184.0000	
	Cache memory used	15,210,842,279.8436	
	Cache memory writes	2,923,301.950	
	Storage driver read requests	243,996.135	
	Storage driver write requests	2,914,623.375	
	System disk bytes read	5,726,920,433	
	System disk bytes written	0.000	
	System disk reads	151,310.405	
	System disk writes	0.000	

Disk write/delete reduction (min/max) – 991,700,688/1,024,606,909,574=-0.001 (over 999%)
Disk writes total reduction – 3,565/1,159,724=-0.0031 (700%)

The thing to notice is how drastically the Disk to Memory ratios are different. This indicates how often the changes made stay in RAM. Just by going from 2 GB to 6 GB we saw a shift from 14:1 to 2:1. When I saw that, I was pleased about it, but I had a feeling we could do better. So, I calculated how much RAM the hosts could handle per VM (see Chapter 3) and increased to 16 GB cache. It was then not only did I see a reduction but a reversal of 1:81. That means that for every byte written to disk, 81 were performed in memory! That's about a 1000% performance difference per VM. Apply this same configuration to all of your CVAD VMs, and you have a winning combination!

The second metric is the one that truly seemed to impact performance for this customer: reducing the overall WRITES. A 700% improvement is what freed up the resources for everything else on the SAN! You should also note that in ALL cases, writes are averted at a minimum of 2:1. Why is that? The customer is using an Internet Explorer-based product that generates a lot of small temporary files that are deleted after use. This means that most of the individual write operations were happening in RAM.

The lesson here- sometimes it's not about the amount of data itself, but the overall number of individual read/write requests. Some refer to this "a death by a thousand cuts," and quite often SAN providers will misrepresent how much IOPS can be handled vs. handled without slowdowns. Sometimes you need data!

How well did it work?
Here's a before and after:

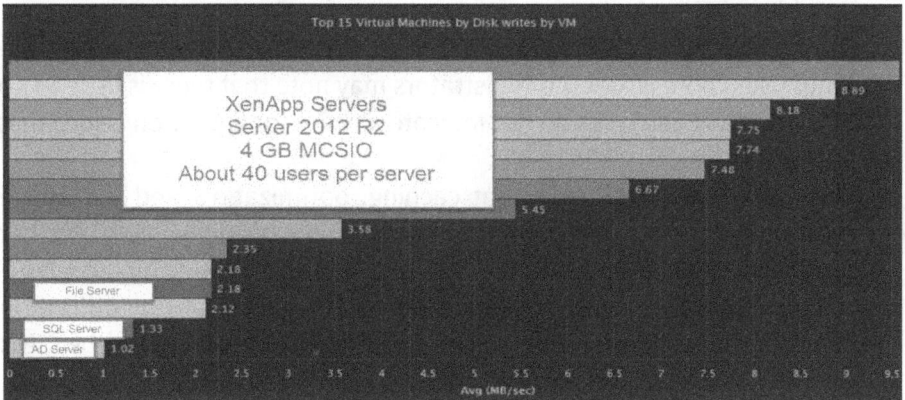

Figure 6: Disk Writes Before Tuning

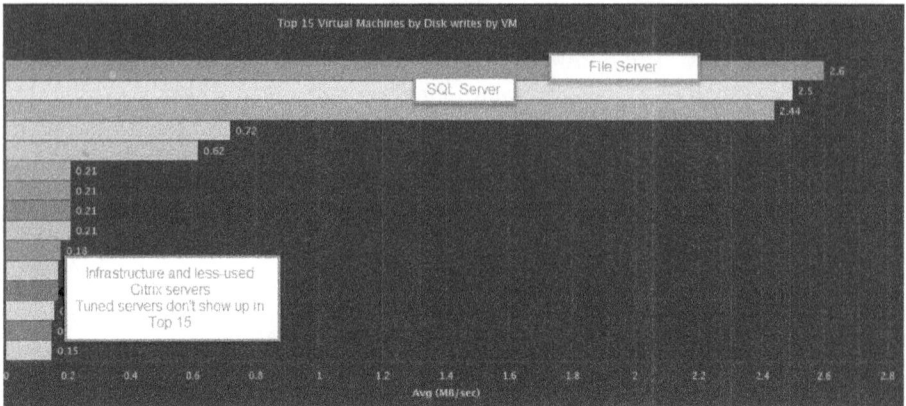

Figure 7: Disk Writes after Tuning

PVS Server Performance Tuning

Problem 2 – PVS Target Device (VDAs) lock-up randomly or are slow at times

Problem Description
PVS Target devices were correctly configured with enough Cache, optimizations, etc. Users are noting apparent lock-ups that clear after a few seconds. Programs are sometimes slow to load, especially early in the mornings. The problems are often much worse after new vDisk versions are deployed.

Troubleshooting Notes
Monitoring the VDAs indicates no unusual CPU activity- in fact, at the times users note issues, Administrators may note that there is little to no CPU activity. Event logs do not indicate any OS configuration issues that are related.

The Citrix team confirmed that caching, optimization, and the above recommendations have been configured properly. By further troubleshooting, they found that many VDAs are indicating high retries.

Network Engineers note there are no packet loss issues or utilization issues on the network (note- be careful here; I have seen would-be Citrix Heroes not accept this explanation and blame the Network, only to be later embarrassed by the real cause).

Background: How the PVS Server *really* works

PVS (again, I'm simplifying here) takes a flat Microsoft VHD file and streams its contents on-demand to a virtually unlimited number of Target Devices. The mechanics of this are important to understand from a performance perspective. It is also important to realize that it is mostly the Microsoft technology that matters for performance. Here's how it works.

As data is read from the flattened VHD + VHDX deltas (versions) the PVS software creates a virtual iSCSI block storage device 'image' which is read via the network much in the same way that would happen if you were to boot a machine from the SAN (yes, people used to do that when storage was more expensive.)

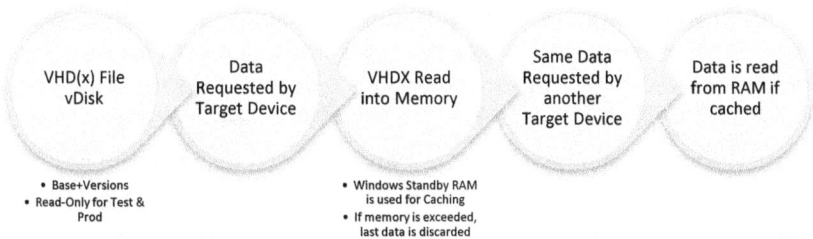

| VHD(x) File vDisk | Data Requested by Target Device | VHDX Read into Memory | Same Data Requested by another Target Device | Data is read from RAM if cached |

- Base+Versions
- Read-Only for Test & Prod

- Windows Standby RAM is used for Caching
- If memory is exceeded, last data is discarded

Figure 8: The PVS Memory Caching Process

The data is streamed via UDP for efficient transport. And when I say efficient, I do mean just that. Contrary to what is often thought- ONLY the data requested is streamed as it is required. This means that during boot- each VM will only need that data which is required- depending on the OS and what loads at startup this may only be a few hundred MB. However, from the server perspective, the key here is that the same data is being read multiple times. A key feature of Windows since Server 2008 has been that reads from both the local hard disk and from SMB shares are both cached in RAM for faster re-reads. PVS takes full advantage here, in this scenario.

(A note on caching of SMB shares: Recent testing has shown that this is difficult to track and that there may be scenarios where this caching is not occurring as we expect. If you want to be sure it is working, we'll discuss some ways of determining that later in this chapter. While I personally like using SMB shares as it reduces overhead and complexity – the sure thing is to store your vDisks on storage local to the PVS server.)

The data is read once from the vDisk and then subsequent re-reads come from RAM. In case you didn't know- reading from RAM is way faster than reading from disk.

Now we put together the READS being very fast from RAM and (from the previous section) WRITES being very fast to RAM... and you've got a winning combination. Now, multiply this by a few thousand VDAs and you can see why I like PVS as a technology a LOT.

But what happens when the reads are NOT coming from RAM, and most, if not all requests have to be re-read from the vDisk store? What this tends to look like from a user experience point of view is that the VM will occasionally slow down significantly. It may even seem to freeze if conditions are poor enough. This will often seem to be CPU related and there is no obvious indicator. On older hardware PCs, this used to be indicated by a 'drive indicator' – which as it turns out does not indicate drive activity but that the OS is waiting for the drive to give it data so it can continue. In this case, the PVS software waits for a response and when it does not get it, it initiates a Retry. Remember that this is a UDP-based stream, but the target device software knows when data is missing and will ask again. And again. And again. This is called a Retry in the PVS console as well and is fortunately recorded by the software. It can be displayed in two places; on the VM itself, but also more importantly on the PVS Console. This is important because you'll be able to see trends of increasing retries across multiple VMs that indicates network troubles. However, more often in modern environments with fast and reliable networks, issues with the PVS server not being able to handle the read demands of the VMs attached cause the retries to occur.

Unfortunately, the response to this is quite often to think that faster storage is needed. As you've probably guessed by now, that is not true.

As you read in the story I told in this chapter's intro, this is more often caused by a lack of memory for Windows to cache in its standby memory.

Memory Sizing

There has been a longtime guidance of where to begin with memory sizing that looks like this:

- Reserve about 4 GB for the Operating System
- Add about 2 GB for each Desktop OS vDisk
- Add about 4 GB for each Server OS vDisk (this has recently been increased to 5 GB)
- Pad by around 15-20% of the resultant vDisk RAM total
- I will add that with PVS versioning, you should add development/testing vDisks into the mix. I find the average amount is about 1 GB per vDisk version active

A few notes on this that are important to know:

- These should be considered a MINIMUM value
- Remember that these calculations are for actively streamed vDisks. This means if you are streaming additional versions, test disks or previous versions that are in transition. This means you need to be aware of how many vDisks are actively being streamed.
- All PVS servers must have enough RAM to cover all vDisk streams.
- Minimize the services running on the server and always make sure that ONLY the PVS services are run on the server. This is especially true of heavy services like SQL.
- Be careful with Antivirus scans – remember that the cache is affected by reads, and it's first in first out (FIFO). So… if your AV is scanning files they will be in RAM at an order that won't really benefit repeat reads; they would have to be re-cached. While not the end of the world once a week or so, if this happens frequently, it can impact performance.

This has been more or less true for nearly a decade now. Dan Allen had a great article about this that really helped nail down how to use the Standby RAM cache properly (archived, but you can find it at CTX125126 if you have a MyCitrix logon). In fact, I remember that prompted by a huge customer's concern having a conversation with Martin Zugec about this after his article in 2012. After some further conversations with Martin, Dan, Pablo, Nick Rintalan and others in Citrix Consulting (where I was serving at the time) some further guidance that I mention below comes

65

into play. I am not willing to take any real credit because so many more talented folks than me were involved and all I was doing was implementing other's ideas. I'll just simply outline what I have personally seen work. I will, however, say aside from the Citrix VDI Handbook, you owe it to yourself to read part 2 "How to Properly Size Your Memory" for a deep dive. All three are linked at https://ctxpro.com/CHlinks/#32.

Here's what I do to make sure my PVS Servers have the right amount of RAM.
First, I start with the same formula.
Let's say, for example, I have two production Windows 10 vDisks that I know I'll always have at least one test or development version active (as in being streamed to a maintenance VM in read-write). I also have five Server 2016 images serving Desktops & Apps. At least three of those will be active for testing development versions. I'm running Server 2016 as a base for my PVS servers.

OS RAM + [{(number of Desktop OS x 2 GB)+(active Dev Versions x 1 GB)+(number of Server OS x 5 GB)+(active Dev Versions x 1 GB)}*15%] = **PVS RAM Requirement**

4 GB for PVS Server 2016 OS + [{(2x2 GB for Windows 10 = 4 GB) + (1x1GB for Desktop Dev= 1 GB) +(5x5 GB for Server OS= 25) + (3x1 GB for Server Dev= 3 GB)}*15%]= **42 GB**.

To break that middle section down:
{(2x2GB)+(1x1GB)+(5x5GB)+(3x1GB)}
{4+1+25+3=33}

[33x15%=4.95 (rounded up as 5)]

4+[33+5]=42

As always, test this out to make sure. Many things can affect how much data is being read from the vDisk store!

Monitoring RAM Used by PVS

Once your server is online and in production, it is important to monitor to make sure that reads are happening from Standby RAM instead of disk. Fortunately, there's a handy Performance Monitor metric for just this!

What you'll want to do is monitor for about 24 hours or more and then parse the results.

The first metrics we are concerned with for this test are Bytes sent/sec on the network interface and Copy Read Hits %.

Optionally, you may also want to include data of when your PVS vDisk store is being read from. This can be either from the network if you are using an HA SMB store, or Logical Disk if you are using local storage (note- if you are using local, I highly recommend using a completely dedicated disk- no system files, no page file, no Cache on Server files – just VHDs.

I tend to keep my metrics simple- at least when I'm analyzing them.

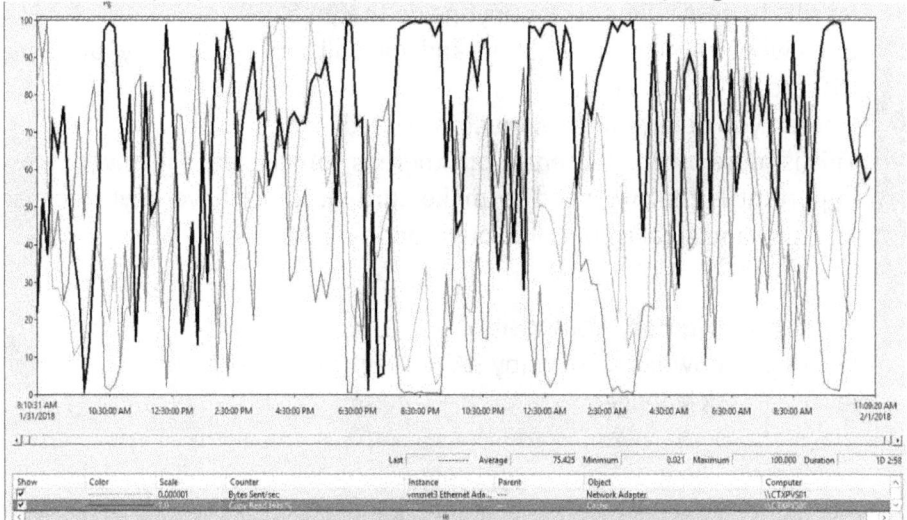

Figure 9: Performance Monitor Output with Cache Read Hits %

The highlighted (black) line here indicates the Cache Read Hits %. The Green is Bytes Sent/sec. Ideally, we want to see the Cache above 80% whenever data is being sent.

*My rule is simple: Whenever PVS is sending Data (bytes
sent) it should correspond to Copy Read Hits % being
above 80%*

Citrix did release an article on this in 2018 on the subject - I'll say here that
it is a huge read, of which the summary backed by my observations is this:
When this value stays above 80% performance is best. If you're familiar
with the law of diminishing returns – this is true of insisting to keep above
80% as well. In other words, spending a lot of effort to get to 90% or 95%
consistently may not be worth the time it takes to get there.
https://ctxpro.com/CHlinks/#33

You may find that you have more memory than you need. In that case, I
leave it to you to decide whether to reduce your server's RAM or not (but
let's be honest… when does anyone do that, really?).
But – what if you've done all this and you still see retries and your Cache
Hits are still below 80%?
How do you determine how much you need in total?
This is more art than science, but there is some science involved. Most
important is that we need to make sure we don't have anything else
cheating and stealing our precious standby RAM!

Looking at Memory Composition

Looking at how much Standby RAM is fairly easy to determine at a high
level via Task Manager.

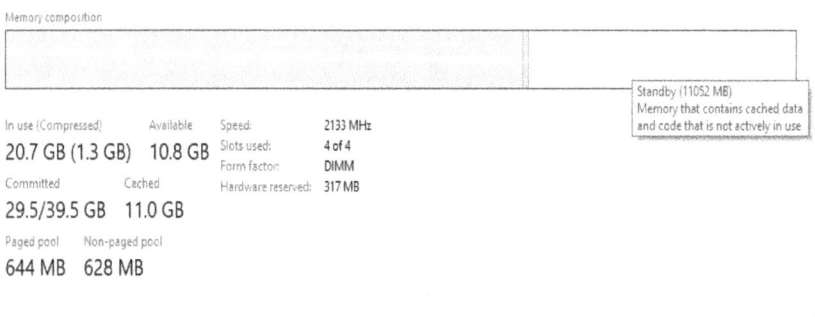

Memory composition

In use (Compressed)	Available	Speed:	2133 MHz
20.7 GB (1.3 GB)	10.8 GB	Slots used:	4 of 4
		Form factor:	DIMM
Committed	Cached	Hardware reserved:	317 MB
29.5/39.5 GB	11.0 GB		
Paged pool	Non-paged pool		
644 MB	628 MB		

Standby (11052 MB)
Memory that contains cached data
and code that is not actively in use

Figure 10: Task Manager Memory Consumption Example

Diving into Resource Monitor you'll see something like this:

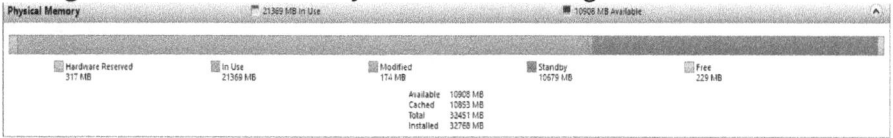

Physical Memory		21369 MB In Use		10908 MB Available		^
Hardware Reserved 317 MB	In Use 21369 MB	Modified 174 MB	Standby 10679 MB	Free 229 MB		

Available 10908 MB
Cached 10853 MB
Total 32451 MB
Installed 32768 MB

Figure 11: Resource Manager Memory Display

OH MY GOODNESS- I ONLY HAVE 229 MB MEMORY FREE! AAAAHHH!
Don't panic. "Free" is not our concern. In fact, there's something key to note here:

Free Memory is Wasted Memory

You want to make practical use of RAM, not have it sitting around doing nothing! With Standby (cached) RAM, we're doing just that.
The dark blue value for Standby indicates all the program and disk reads that are cached into RAM. That's why it is vital not to simply size based on just your PVS's requirements but EVERYTHING that is required. Determining this more precisely will often take diving in a bit further. I have typically used a Microsoft Sysinternals tool called "RAMMAP" to determine how much of a file is in active vs standby RAM.
Remember that just because you have a 120 GB vDisk that not all of that size needs to be cached. You may find, in most cases, that drastically less of that data needs to be cached.
Or sometimes more. Here's a real-world example of what this may look like:

Path		Total	Standby	Modified	Modified No-Write	Active
E:\	_v1.vhdx	13,510,712 K	12,139,048 K			1,371,664 K
E:\	_v1.4.pvp	4 K				4 K
E:\	_v1.4.lok	4 K	4 K			
E:\	_v1.4.avhdx	1,452,692 K	1,208,052 K			244,640 K
E:\	_v1.3.avhdx	381,900 K	284,244 K			97,656 K
E:\	_v1.2.avhdx	50,956 K	2,740 K			48,216 K
E:\	_v1.1.avhdx	745,784 K	623,340 K			122,444 K
E:\	_v2.9.avhd	21,004 K				21,004 K
E:\	_v2.8.avhd	13,240 K				13,240 K
E:\	_v2.7.avhd	13,664 K				13,664 K
E:\	_v2.6.vhd	292,008 K				292,008 K
E:\	_v2.12.pvp	192 K				192 K
E:\	_v2.12.avhd	204,860 K	360 K			204,500 K
E:\	_v2.11.avhd	21,396 K	4 K			21,392 K
E:\	_v2.10.avhd	20,760 K				20,760 K
E:\	_v4.9.avhdx	15,660 K	80 K			15,580 K
E:\	_v4.8.avhdx	32,436 K	4,644 K			27,792 K
E:\	_v4.7.avhdx	11,996 K	16 K			11,980 K
E:\	_v4.6.vhdx	378,128 K	131,868 K			246,260 K
E:\	_v4.11.avhdx	214,876 K	23,060 K			191,816 K
E:\	_v4.10.avhdx	25,240 K	88 K			25,152 K
E:\\denle...lv.701747..'2.9.avhdx		55,332 K				55,332 K
E:\	2.8.avhdx	9,796 K				9,796 K
E:\	2.7.avhdx	233,804 K				233,804 K
E:\	2.6.vhdx	473,540 K				473,540 K
E:\	2.14.avhdx	196,484 K				196,484 K
E:\	2.13.pvp	4 K				4 K
E:\	2.13.avhdx	227,776 K				227,776 K
E:\	2.12.avhdx	107,872 K				107,872 K
E:\	2.11.avhdx	76,988 K				76,988 K
E:\......._.2.10.avhdx		92,740 K				92,740 K
E:\s		4 K	4 K			
E:\$recycle.bin\s-1-5-21-89 1056679-1315381286-200095...		4 K	4 K			
C:\windows\winsxs\x86_microsoft.windows.common-cont...		420 K	216 K			204 K
C:\windows\winsxs\manifests\x86_microsoft.windows.sys...		4 K	4 K			
C:\windows\winsxs\manifests\x86_microsoft.windows.isol...		4 K	4 K			
C:\windows\winsxs\manifests\x86_microsoft.windows.i..u...		4 K	4 K			
C:\windows\winsxs\manifests\x86_microsoft.windows.gdi...		4 K	4 K			
C:\windows\winsxs\manifests\x86_microsoft.windows.co...		4 K	4 K			
C:\windows\winsxs\manifests\x86_microsoft.windows.co...		4 K	4 K			

Figure 12: Example of RAMMap on a PVS Server

You can see here that as Windows reads files, it will place portions of the file in Standby RAM and portions in Active RAM. PVS software doesn't control this, remember, so if you have more than PVS functions going on in your server... it can be a factor!

The second factor is, of course, the amount of data being read. Just because the guidance is 5 GB for server OS, for example, I have seen scenarios where well over 12 GB needs to be cached. It depends on the application and other data that must be read during the machine's lifecycle.

This is often true with environments with higher than average (or needed) images. Unfortunately, in recent cases, this has been seen with App Layering. Remember- vDisks are cached individually. Even if they are built from the same base and send identical, they still consume RAM individually. Sorry.

But this is also true of other reads! So if you have other programs that read data from the disk (like Antivirus, etc) you may find yourself consuming more than intended.

In summary:
One of the most common causes of retries is the PVS server not being able to meet read requests rapidly enough. Typically, this is caused by inadequate RAM on the PVS Server. When vDisks are read, Windows Server will automatically cache the data. This reduces reads from disk because the non-persistent VMs are always reading the same data. However, because the cache is FIFO (First In First Out) if the amount of read data exceeds the cache, the PVS server must read from its vDisk Store. Even with very fast storage, seek times and transfer can cause delays.
Citrix has guidance on how to get started with proper RAM sizing for PVS. A common misconception is that it would be better to have faster storage- in fact, some customers use physical hardware or dedicated Flash-Based or RAM-Based storage only to find that the improvement is minimal. RAM is a far cheaper solution.

Solutions to Test
Here's your tasks for this, with a few caveats:
1. All PVS servers should be identical in every way possible
2. PVS servers can definitely be virtual (better this way, IMO) but you should be careful not to run additional services on them
3. Though RAM can be added to most VMs (including PVS servers) without a reboot, scheduling an outage is still a good idea when making any changes to a production system
4. Data has to be read the first time before it can be cached – so keep in mind that the first time you read a vDisk or version it may take some time to 'warm up'- this is why I recommend at least 24 hrs of data be analyzed.

Overall- the goals for this should be to reduce retries and disk read IO from the PVS server.

EXERCISE
1) RECORD THE CURRENT IOPS FOR THE PVS SERVER, AND TAKE SPECIAL NOTE OF READ IOPS
2) RECORD THE CURRENT USAGE OF STANDBY RAM
3) SET UP AT LEAST 24 HRS OF PERFORMANCE MONITOR
    a. CACHE HITS %
    b. NETWORK DATA SENT (BYTES/SEC)
    c. DISK READ (BYTES/SEC)
    d. NETWORK READ BYTES/SEC IF USING SMB FILESHARES
4) USE RAMMAP TO 'SNAPSHOT' THE CURRENT STATUS OF CACHING CONFIGURATION
5) 24 HRS LATER- EXAMINE THE PERFORMANCE MONITOR REPORT
    a. HOW MANY TIMES DOES THE CACHE DROP BELOW 80% *AND* BYTES ARE BEING SENT?
    b. ARE THERE TIMES OF HEAVY READS THAT INDICATE A PROCESS MAY BE LOADING MEMORY INTO CACHE BUT IS NOT SENDING DATA TO THE NETWORK? (IF SO- CONSIDER RUNNING THE MONITOR FOR A WEEK TO IDENTIFY A PATTERN). IF THIS IS A RECURRING PATTERN, BEST TO SOLVE THIS BEFORE MOVING ON
6) COUNT YOUR ACTIVE VDISKS – HINT: YOU CAN TELL PVS IS STREAMING A VDISK IN THE CONSOLE BY LOOKING FOR THE 'LOCK' ICON IN THE VDISKS VIEW.
7) USE THE BASE FORMULA TO DETERMINE THE ESTIMATED RAM REQUIREMENTS:
    4 GB FOR WINDOWS + [{(N*2 GB FOR WINDOWS 10) + (N*1GB FOR DESKTOP VERSIONS) +(N*5 GB FOR SERVER OS) + (N*1 GB FOR SERVER DEV)}*15%]= _____
    a. IS YOUR PVS SERVER BELOW THE RAM ESTIMATE NEEDED? BY HOW MUCH?
    b. IF YOUR SERVER IS ABOVE YOUR ESTIMATE AND IS STILL HAVING RETRIES USE RAMMAP TO DETERMINE HOW MUCH OF EACH FILE IS BEING READ. I WOULD RECOMMEND GATHERING 1-2 DAYS OF RESULTS AFTER A REBOOT BY CHECKING RAMMAP EVERY 3-4 HOURS AND COMPARING THE RESULTS. YOU ARE LOOKING FOR PATTERNS OF NEW DATA OVERWRITING OLDER DATA (FIFO). TRY TO

ESTIMATE HOW MUCH RAM WOULD BE NEEDED TO PREVENT THIS *OR* TRY TO REDUCE THE READS OVERALL.

8) INCREASE THE RAM OF YOUR SERVERS BY THE VALUE NOTED ABOVE
   a. INCREASE TO THAT VALUE FOR ALL SERVERS
   b. RE-RUN THE PERFORMANCE MONITOR STEP FOR AT LEAST 24-48 HOURS.

9) REPEAT THE STEPS UNTIL YOU HAVE A CONSISTENT 80% OR MORE CACHE HITS PERCENTAGE. REMEMBER – WE ARE JUST CONCERNED ABOUT WHEN DATA IS BEING SENT OUT SO YOU'LL RARELY SEE A 100% VALUE THE WHOLE TIME.

10) EVERY SO OFTEN (MONTHLY IS IDEAL BUT QUARTERLY IS OKAY TOO) MAKE SURE YOU RUN THE TESTS AGAIN TO IDENTIFY CACHE MISSES. THIS PROACTIVE MAINTENANCE CAN GO A LONG WAY TO ASSURING YOUR LONG TIME LOVE AFFAIR WITH PVS!

Chapter 5: Active Directory for Virtual Apps and Desktops

"But, we've always done it this way, and it's always worked!"

When Microsoft debuted Active Directory some 19 years prior to me writing this, I will admit I didn't realize just how important it would become… and how behind people would stay when it comes to Virtual Apps and Desktops.

What I am seeing in the field today indicates not only a lack of understanding of how AD works but the worse understanding of the more crucial component – Group Policy. I am still finding logon scripts (many of which don't even work, just waste logon times trying to) and policies applied very badly. These bad policies often linger because the team managing Active Directory does not understand a crucial concept: What works well for a Desktop in a cubicle is very likely not to work well when you apply the same policies to a user logging onto a Server OS VDA. Perhaps worse than that is when said team does not realize that the user policies applied must be as well-designed as the computer policies. This chapter will arm you with what you need to know to be able to speak authoritatively to how it should be done and why! We'll be drawing from Citrix Consulting's guidance as well as top experts.

Layers	• **User**
	• **Control**
Success Lanes	• Design
	• Build
Prerequisites	• Windows Desktop and Server OS Knowledge
	• Active Directory
Importance	🎸 🎸 🎸 🎸
User Impact	🎸 🎸 🎸 🎸

Security Impact	🎸 🎸 🎸
Difficulty	🎸 🎸

Key Concepts

First and foremost -

There is no perfect Active Directory design. There is only understanding what has worked best for others, then designing what works for your unique environment. In other words, it is better to emulate before you innovate with the understanding that you will very rarely be able to do so perfectly. The truth is they didn't either.

Opinions are like feet. We will all typically have them, and they can all stink from time to time. This is also true of opinions regarding Active Directory and Group Policy design. All I'm asking is that you trust the collective experience here and if you need to form your own opinion, make sure it is based on current reality, not past experiences. Being stuck in the past, you can very likely miss things that change based on use cases and technical requirements beyond to which you are accustomed. Because it worked once does NOT mean it will work again. Assumption is the most dangerous negative force in all of Information Technology.

Assumption is the most dangerous negative force in all of Information Technology

I'm also acutely aware that many if not most of my readers will not be in direct control of their Active Directory infrastructure. Further, I'm also very aware of how often this can cause conflicts and heated discussions among IT teams. I would have you consider that the reasons for what I lay out here are to make for a better and more secure user environment with faster logon times and more granular management. Contrary to what some AD Administrators seem to believe- we aren't trying to make their life more difficult and give

75

them more objects to manage just because we are being territorial or difficult. There genuinely are drastically different considerations for a virtual user environment, especially when using apps and desktops from a Server OS.

In the Citrix realm – easily the most important thing to remember is that you need to know that a shocking number of outages are caused when policies that work for other servers or desktop OS components are applied to Citrix servers. These are often applied with the best of intentions, security being an especially common justification. For this reason, the very first concept is to dedicate OUs to Citrix. The second is to block policy inheritance. Third, be aware that forced inheritance from the top level of a domain (especially modifying the Default Domain policy) can be very dangerous to the stability of Citrix Virtual Apps and Desktops. I wish I had a count of the number of times I was called to an organization to determine what was wrong with Citrix only to determine that the issue was a change made by other Active Directory admins that the team either didn't know about or didn't realize would cause an impact. I can think of five of eight in 2019 alone. Surely you can imagine that this has happened frequently over the last 15 years. What alarms me is that it is happening more instead of less – a significant driver for getting this chapter written.

If you read nothing else in this chapter, please understand these things:
- Assumption is the most dangerous negative force in all of Information Technology and is more apparent in Group Policy.
- Isolate All Citrix infrastructure and workloads as much as possible from others in the organization. Get exceptions to legacy mandates such as grouping all Servers in an OU.
- Maintain dedicated copies of policies applied to other servers in the datacenter.
- Test Policy changes separately from other use cases. Never assume what has no effect in one area will not affect Citrix.
- Choose simplicity whenever possible. Just don't compromise security to make it simple.
- Make every attempt to consolidate policies, but only do so when it will not present Operational or User experience challenges.

- Choose your battles. Active Directory is the most contended battleground in IT save for the Hypervisor.

Reference Infrastructure – Active Directory OUs and GPOs

A little unusual for me, in this case, is *not to start with why,* but to start by showing you what I typically recommend. These recommendations are backed by nearly two decades of experience and working with Citrix Consulting, top organizations, and architects worldwide.

Here is the reference organization that myself and others at Citrix have used effectively. I've made a few updates given some more modern considerations, including a more frequent use of Resource domains and Federation. This used to be more complicated. Your goal should be keeping it simple!

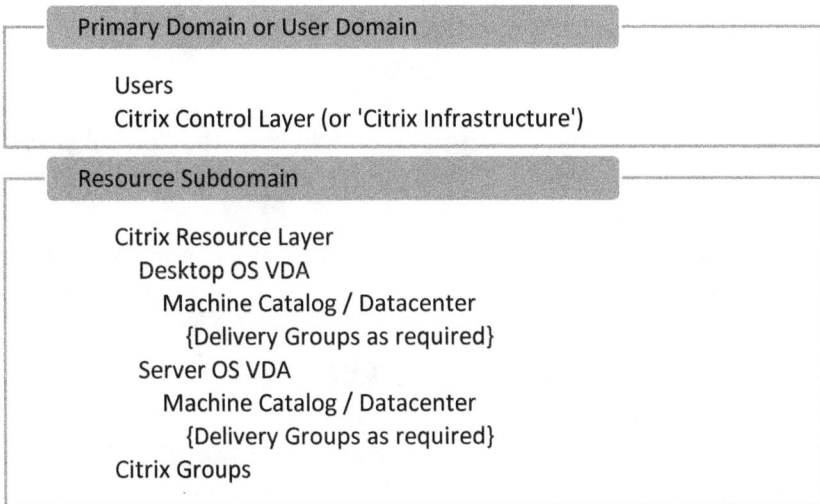

Primary Domain or User Domain

    Users
    Citrix Control Layer (or 'Citrix Infrastructure')

Resource Subdomain

    Citrix Resource Layer
      Desktop OS VDA
        Machine Catalog / Datacenter
          {Delivery Groups as required}
      Server OS VDA
        Machine Catalog / Datacenter
          {Delivery Groups as required}
    Citrix Groups

Note that some organizations will want to start with a "Citrix" OU and break out the subcomponents from there. I like to keep the depth of the OUs to a minimum. But sometimes you need to get along with others, and this is not a hill on which to die.

Nonetheless, these require quite a bit of explanation. Let's break this down a bit.

Control Layer (Infrastructure)

Just in case you are not yet familiar, the Citrix Control layer is the components used to control and deliver the VDAs. Though I used to separate the Access components, I find these days that there are rarely policies that can't be applied to all if any are required at all. Back before Server 2012 we very often had to create separate OUs for the application of GPOs to optimize the OS for services like PVS – however, these are so rare now that I think all these components can be housed within the Control or Infrastructure OU. You can name it either way; they both make sense.

Just avoid having your Citrix control and access components subject to other server OUs or policies. You do want to be in control over policies applied, and per our first practice, never assume that policies that are fine for other servers are okay for Citrix control or resource servers. It is better to make a copy of a Server policy for Citrix Infrastructure and maintain (read: test) it separately than to have an outage because all of your VDAs can't contact your controllers suddenly. If it hasn't happened more than once, I wouldn't call it out so specifically!

The question then is what Citrix servers should be in the Control Layer? More or less, everything that isn't a VDA! Here's what I usually consider:

- Delivery Controllers
- Cloud Connectors (including Endpoint Management and other connectors)
- Provisioning Services (PVS)
- Federated Authentication Service (FAS)
- Workspace Environment Management (WEM)
- StoreFront (could be considered part of the Access Layer, but for AD purposes we put it here)
- Director
- ShareFile Connector or Storage Zone Controller (Citrix Collaboration)

Resource Layer

Serving the user is the job of the Resource layer. These are the servers and desktop OS machines users will be logging onto and with which they will be interacting. So, your Resource Layer OUs should contain all of your

Virtual Delivery Agents (VDAs), and possibly other associated resources such as mobile.

- Desktop OS VDAs
- Remote PC VDAs
- Server OS VDAs

OU Structure

So how will you end up structuring this?

I've most commonly seen AD teams wanting the Citrix Infrastructure to all be in one nested OU. But then they often complain about having too many OU's deep.

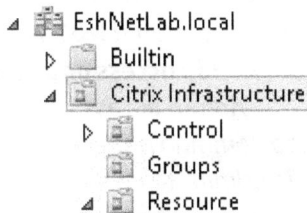

Figure 13: Nested OU Option

But it often makes sense to separate these items out for top-level administration and for keeping the overall OU depth even lower. For this you may need an expanded Nest:

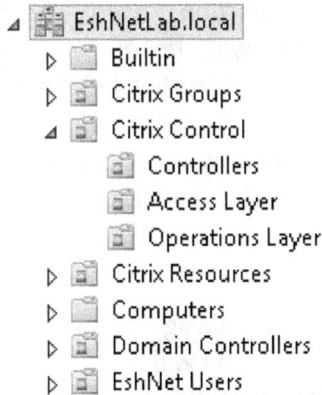

Figure 14: Expanded Nested OU Option

What you should avoid, however – is the mistake of putting Citrix OUs under "Server" or "Computers" OUs. While this may be the norm at your organization, I have seen far too many disasters in this arena when

79

someone decides to enforce a security policy on all "Servers" that suddenly cause the Citrix Controllers to stop being able to handle logons.

WHY SEPARATE OUS?

I recommend having not only dedicated OUs to the Citrix Infrastructure but also dedicated permissions that allow Enterprise Admin but block other Domain Admins. This management restriction allows you to add the Citrix Service account and the Citrix Engineers and Admins to be able to manage machine accounts and policies (objects) exclusively.
A crucial reason for this is that you'll NOT want to give your Citrix Service accounts Domain Admin access and certainly not Enterprise Admin access.
In other words, an all-too-common practice of just assigning the Citrix service accounts to domain admins to deal with permissions is risky. What if someone leaves the company and has that account password? What if it is used in documentation or other connection shortcut files that may leave your company? By dedicating a specific OU to which the Citrix Service accounts have permission to make changes to the objects contained there, you are limiting your risk of compromise while still allowing Citrix to function properly.
Conversely, I consider it an operational risk to simply allow "Domain Admins" access to Citrix Administration functions. You only want those with training to be able to access these functions, and the OU structure should be treated the same way. So only add those individuals to your Citrix Admins.

Designing Your OU Structure

It is essential to take your time designing an OU structure. Your primary consideration should be how you will be applying Group Policy Objects (GPOs). The reality is that as a Citrix environment grows and use cases expand, the OU structure can become challenging to manage in a hurry. And since policy differences tend to be the most common reason to isolate Delivery Groups (at least, those that use the same image), sound design upfront is crucial.

Your primary consideration in OU Structure should be how you will be applying Group Policy Objects (GPOs).

I usually recommend that you whiteboard a design with all parties involved.

Then erase the board and re-draw it again. If you draw it twice the same way and everyone is still happy- odds are good you'll have a more future-proof design.

Here's my reference design for an Enterprise OU structure:

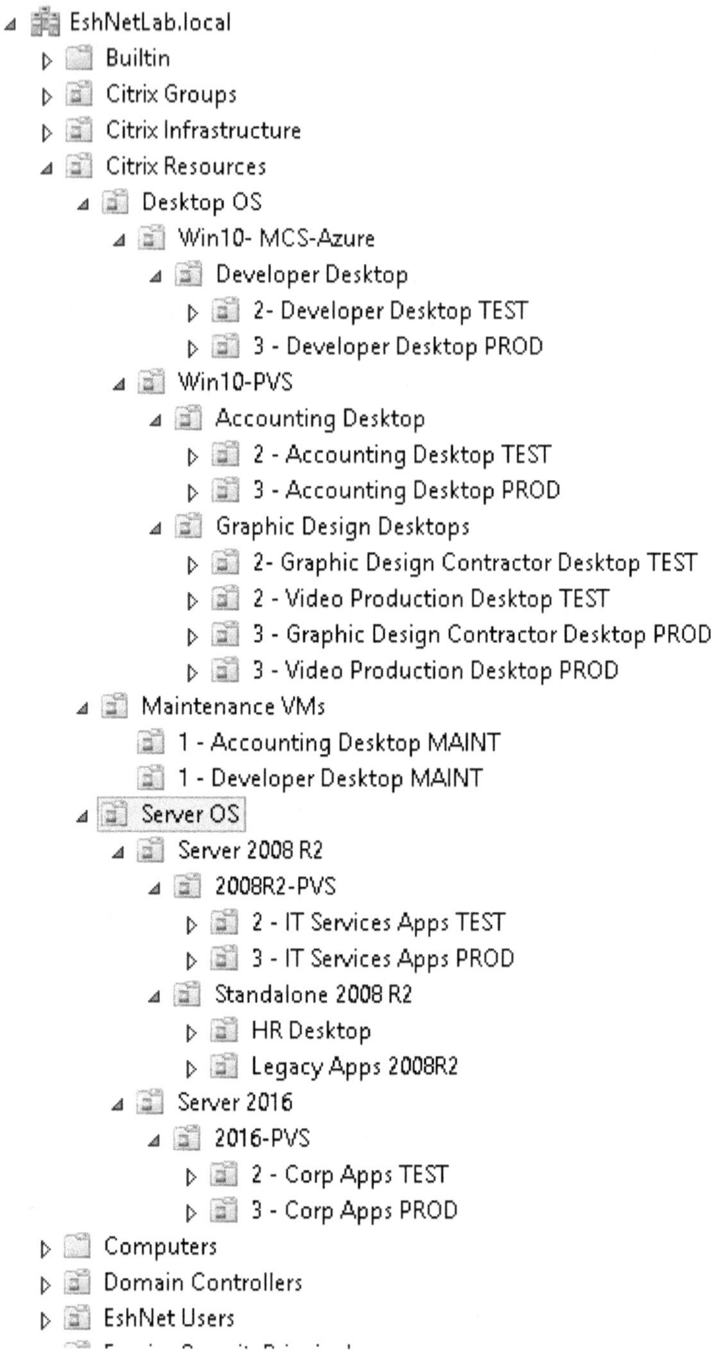

- EshNetLab.local
  - Builtin
  - Citrix Groups
  - Citrix Infrastructure
  - Citrix Resources
    - Desktop OS
      - Win10- MCS-Azure
        - Developer Desktop
          - 2- Developer Desktop TEST
          - 3 - Developer Desktop PROD
      - Win10-PVS
        - Accounting Desktop
          - 2 - Accounting Desktop TEST
          - 3 - Accounting Desktop PROD
        - Graphic Design Desktops
          - 2- Graphic Design Contractor Desktop TEST
          - 2 - Video Production Desktop TEST
          - 3 - Graphic Design Contractor Desktop PROD
          - 3 - Video Production Desktop PROD
      - Maintenance VMs
        - 1 - Accounting Desktop MAINT
        - 1 - Developer Desktop MAINT
    - Server OS
      - Server 2008 R2
        - 2008R2-PVS
          - 2 - IT Services Apps TEST
          - 3 - IT Services Apps PROD
        - Standalone 2008 R2
          - HR Desktop
          - Legacy Apps 2008R2
      - Server 2016
        - 2016-PVS
          - 2 - Corp Apps TEST
          - 3 - Corp Apps PROD
  - Computers
  - Domain Controllers
  - EshNet Users

Figure 15: Reference AD OU Configuration

You'll notice that I organize by Overall Function, then OS, then either Machine Catalog (note the Imaging Mechanism or Datacenter location is sometimes noted here) or Delivery Groups. This allows for machine images and policies to be linked/shared effectively while still allowing granular control where it needs to be. Again- you never want to rely on WMI processing for User logons. Better to control the policies users are getting by OU + User Group contexts in the policy itself.

You'll also notice the numbers in front of certain OUs. This is a system I've used for the last few years to easily distinguish OUs (and also Delivery Groups and Machine names) in their workflow position.

1. Maintenance Cycle
2. Test Cycle
3. Production
4. Quality Assurance / Patch testing

I find that making these distinctions (and making them CONSISTENT) makes overall Administration much easier to handle because everyone is on the same page.

Before I walk you through the logic, I use for my OUs under Resource, note again that this is the area of the strongest "it depends" you may ever see. But remember, your goal here is to apply as few Group Policy Objects (GPOs) as possible for the quickest logon – but probably more importantly for the most granular balance between that and administrative effort.

While the very fastest logon would likely be a single GPO applied to the VDA, this is not practical in pretty much every case I have ever seen. The more Delivery Groups you have with more individual needs, the more you would have to update GPOs for each of these with the same settings when changes are required.

Group Policy Objects (GPOs)

Easily the most potent aspect of Active Directory is without a doubt Group Policy Objects. The power to apply settings for user experience, security, and machine operating rules based on a context is where GPOs shine. Applied to your choice of User or Computer contexts, they are significant enough that I have quite literally never seen a Citrix design that can exist without them. If you haven't guessed, I have also quite literally seen hundreds of Citrix designs since 2005 when I started focusing on Citrix.

Nested Design

Again thanks to my friend Nick Rintalan from Citrix, I will forever have the game Plinko stuck in my mind.

Plinko was one of the games on the CBS show "The Price is Right," where a player drops a puck at the top of the game, and it bounces off of pegs on its way down... landing eventually on prizes, cash - or nothing.

Figure 16: Plinko on The Price Is Right

Nick described the application of policy in an End User Computing environment like watching the game play out. You start with a baseline policy, then as your context is further defined you will get other policies applied to you based on criteria like the machine you are logging into, your user account (and groups to which you belong), your method of access, and perhaps your physical location. Each of these context shifts represent a bounce to a new policy setting that impacts the outcome to the user session.

So how do you organize these various rules and contexts? To best accommodate current and future needs, I recommend what I call a 'nested' GPO design. This is accomplished by setting baseline policies with settings common to all, then filtered exceptions for delivery groups, security groups, and then individuals.

This allows you to set up what amounts to rows in the Plinko table:

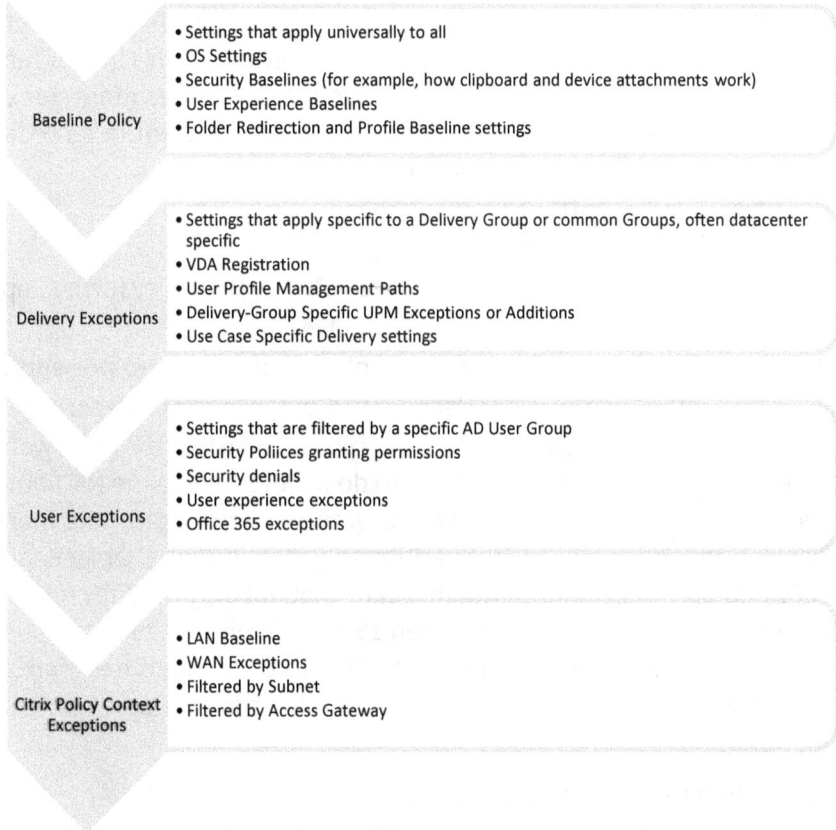

Baseline Policy
- Settings that apply universally to all
- OS Settings
- Security Baselines (for example, how clipboard and device attachments work)
- User Experience Baselines
- Folder Redirection and Profile Baseline settings

Delivery Exceptions
- Settings that apply specific to a Delivery Group or common Groups, often datacenter specific
- VDA Registration
- User Profile Management Paths
- Delivery-Group Specific UPM Exceptions or Additions
- Use Case Specific Delivery settings

User Exceptions
- Settings that are filtered by a specific AD User Group
- Security Poliices granting permissions
- Security denials
- User experience exceptions
- Office 365 exceptions

Citrix Policy Context Exceptions
- LAN Baseline
- WAN Exceptions
- Filtered by Subnet
- Filtered by Access Gateway

Figure 17: How Active Directory Works Like Plinko

What you end up with at the end of your Plinko journey is what is referred to as a "Resultant Set of Policy" (RSOP); the collective result of the policies that are being applied in your context. Though we will talk more about this soon, the key concept here is understanding the importance context plays in the application of policy. A good design will attempt to

85

identify and eliminate redundancy or put settings that apply to all further along in the chain.

So, can you expect to have only 3 GPOs applied to a VDA and then finish with Citrix Policy to control the rest of the user experience? Very rarely. However, by being wise with the application of inheritance, you can have very lightweight GPOs that are processed quickly.

Of course, I'd be remiss if I didn't say right away that where this falls apart in practice for people is when it comes to the way this is displayed in Active Directory. What actually happens in the Group Policy Objects management is that policy is applied from the *bottom up.* This means that when an Active Directory controller is asked to give a Resultant Set of Policy, it is taking the baselines you set and applying them in an order (which you can see in the tab) where this happens:

1. Policies at the bottom are recorded.
2. Policies going up are recorded.
3. Conflicts in the same setting are overruled by the policy further 'up' in the order.
4. The server generates a completed picture of policy and presents a single either Computer or User context to the logon process.

While this process happens quickly, surely you can see that the more work your Active Directory controllers have to do in determining the RSOP the more time your logins will take. Likewise, the more complex, the more work will have to be done. Active Directory Group Policy Objects are ENFORCED at the client level, which means that not only will they refresh at a regular interval (typically between 15 and 45 min) the process must be completed before a logon can occur. Therefore, problems here can be the single most significant cause of delayed logons in your environment. It matters!

The Baseline Consolidation Guideline

As mentioned, you should endeavor to have as few policies as make sense administratively. However, I am a big fan of setting standalone policies for a single setting while they are tested. I won't get into all the theory here, but needless to say, every time you make a change to a GPO, it must then sync a new version of that policy across the SYSVOL folders. While the newer methods of replication are MUCH better than they were, the problem comes in backing out changes for single settings. It is much easier administratively to back out a single policy. So, testing new settings from a standalone GPO makes a lot of sense. What I have been suggesting in recent years is reviewing the exception policies more frequently to see if they can be consolidated into your baselines or into the appropriate exception policies. Do this once the tested settings have been stable for a month or so and you'll have less overall objects to sync, making your AD Administrators happier!

But once again, don't sacrifice operational flexibility for a fraction of a second faster logon speed unless it makes perfect sense.

What about Filtering?

While I'm generally a fan of User Exception policies being filtered by user groups, what I am not a fan of is WMI filtering. Not only does it make administration more difficult instead of less, but it also tends to add to the overall processing time, sometimes by 20 or more seconds, just because WMI is being queried. You'll note from the overall design here that by having OUs per-machine context (Delivery Group) you can filter by users for policies, and you will have covered a good 80% or more of the context desired for most WMI filtered policies I have seen. In other words, WMI filtering becomes a waste of time in nearly every use case!

Processing Order for Policies

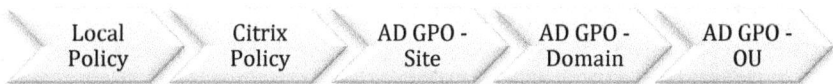

Local Policy	Citrix Policy	AD GPO - Site	AD GPO - Domain	AD GPO - OU

Figure 18: How Policies Are Processed

It is important to remember that Local Policy is read first but can be overruled. Local Policy is NOT enforced- but Active Directory GPOs are. Further, GPOs are typically refreshed, meaning that changes made during the session that conflict with the policy would not stick.

Blocking Inheritance

One of the most essential tools for the Citrix Engineer within Group Policy Objects is the ability to block GPOs above from being applied to OUs within their control. This is important for several reasons.

1. Citrix tends to have needs above and beyond the normal GPOs applied in an organization
2. Citrix VDAs tend to need policies applied in different ways and different test cycles than other GPOs in the organization
3. In my experience, a large number of Citrix outages are caused by either unannounced or 'assumed good' changes to policies that have been either inherited or linked to Citrix OUs.
4. Machines used for imaging should have all policies blocked to avoid the image becoming 'tattooed' with settings. Because the GPO not only writes registry settings but keeps the computer settings in place after logoff, reversing changes made to defaults can be challenging.
5. Security measures such as change monitoring and Antivirus registrations should always be handled differently for Citrix VDAs.
6. Windows Update, Firewall, and Software deployment rules often defined in GPOs should almost always be done differently for Citrix VDAs – re-using the same GPOs as the rest of the organization can be risky.

Often missed is #4 – making sure you have little to no policies applied to your build VMs. What also is very frequently missed is that very often, changes are made to policies that should be tested before putting the changes into production. I will often use blocked inheritance within a TEST OU to assure that we have complete control over the policies that are being tested.

Linked Policies or Copies of Policies?
Another leading practice that is skipped far too often is to have dedicated GPOs for Citrix VDAs. This can get complicated when testing is being performed when you are using the smart nested inheritance I'm suggesting. How do you test changes to a policy without changing it in production? Unfortunately, the answer is you create copies of your GPOs in your test OU – simulate the inheritance order that the production OU would typically have. Then you can track the changes you are making and the impacts they have. Once testing is complete, you'd then have two options:

- Copy the GPO to production and unlink the old policy – this has the advantage of being able to quickly rollback to the previous policy.

However, it does increase the number of GPOs being managed and it is easy to forget to delete the now unused policy once production is stable. I like to set Outlook reminders for myself to delete after a few weeks in the same way I set reminders to consolidate policies.

- Make the same changes in production – This has the advantage of one merely creating a new GPO version, so you don't have to worry about deleting the old one. The disadvantages are that rollback becomes much more difficult, and depending on how many changes you are making, it could represent re-doing much work.

What about Logon Scripts?

Back before Group Policy and before people understood how to manage Group Policy Objects, what we were seeing was settings to control the user environment, security, and even things like mapping drive letters to network shares (yeah, we used to do that with text files, kids!).

Now- if you are still using Logon Scripts at this point, I'd like to remind you that this was always a compromise process from the late 1990s; not the greatest solution for a modern workspace.

Logon Scripts, by merely being called (regardless of what they do), ALWAYS slow down logons to some degree. Scripts like this typically run single-threaded and will, at times, quite literally pause other system processes while they are running. That means when you see a logon 'stuck' and the processor 'pegged' at 25% on a 4 vCPU system? That's very often a logon script.

One of the worst problems with bad Loopback Processing tends to be things like Logon Scripts embedded into policies in the User OU.

I have seen dramatic improvements in environments by setting Loopback to Replace and tracking down any logon scripts. I think my record is finding eight different policies, all with logon scripts – several of which made changes to system files; this in an environment where they thought there was one policy with scripts and couldn't figure out what the issue was. In a Server OS, issues like this can be especially harmful to user logon. In several cases, it causes problems where the script cannot continue because a system file is open, so the user is stuck waiting for the logon processing to time out.

Some of the worst offenders in this regard are drive mappings.

I have seen more slow logons due to flaws in drive
mapping than any other cause of drastically slow
logon times

The problem with mapped drives (other than the thought of why are we still using them, it's not 1988 anymore) is quite often what happens when the server hosting the share is either not present, slow, using legacy SMB, or refuses the connection because of permissions. In that event, each drive mapping must time out before the logon can continue. Those 18-minute logons? Yeah, there's your cause. I bring this up because the overwhelming majority of the times I have found these issues during assessments, there are scripts embedded in Group Policy applied at the user level, and loopback is set to merge (the default).

Loopback Processing

If your domain has multiple use cases using Loopback Processing, it is not a bad idea to create a loopback policy (as in, the loopback rules are the only thing applied in the GPO) and link it to the appropriate OUs. I do encounter plenty of environments where a policy for, say, Internet Explorer also contains a loopback rule. Remember that inheritance order is crucial with policies- and something as important as Loopback Processing should not be in anything but either

a) A specific policy
b) A baseline policy

I prefer a specific policy only for Loopback Processing that is always enforced, placing it to the top. This prevents the scenario like the above, where a policy is linked into the OU without the admins realizing it contains a new Loopback policy that overrides the baseline.

Also of be aware of cross-domain loopback processing. Be very careful of this setting, especially if you are using a resource domain with users in a primary domain. If federation is in use, this won't matter, but I have seen severe problems with long logon times and instability that traced back to the enabling of this setting. I try to avoid it and copy policy settings into my resource domain instead.

Group Policy Preferences

So how do you replace the hassle and slow processing of Logon Scripts? When Microsoft unveiled Group Policy PREFERENCES (GPP), I think people didn't understand the entire benefit. Multi-Threaded, asynchronous processing was just scratching the surface. The real power of the system is that it truly can do the very functions that logon scripts do with more speed and intelligence.

From creating folders on the user's Desktop automatically to mapping drives and printers intelligently – GPP focuses on delivering a contextual user experience better than was previously possible.

I use GPP to do everything from assigning file permissions, publishing icons, and hiding drives higher than D (fun fact- you can 'map' a drive matching your CD ROM drive letter with the 'hidden' attribute in GPP to hide your CD ROM Drive or Cache Drive. This is important for PVS target devices where you don't want users to see the Cache Drive (typically D or E) because the ability to hide drives in Group Policy only goes to D.)

My challenge to those clinging to logon scripts is often to prove to me that they can't do the same thing with GPP. Let's just say I have an excellent win record with this challenge- so with high confidence, I'll issue the same challenge to you!

Regardless- the reason to use GPP has to do with better flexibility, having a graphical interface to accomplish the same tasks as logon scripts, better (and faster) contextual filtering, and a faster logon. In other words, GPP is crucial for Virtual Apps and Desktops!

GPP Tips (from Microsoft)

The following tips are my summary of what Microsoft has to say about GPP performance:

- Foreground processing only occurs when the machine starts up or when the user logs on.
- Client-Side Extensions (CSEs) can only run during foreground processing.
  Folder Redirection
  Group Policy Preferences Drive Mapping.
- Background processing occurs every 90 or so minutes
  GP refreshes itself
  Background processing happens in the background
  While background processing doesn't impact performance, **foreground processing can extend start and logon times**.

- Default Processing has been Asynchronous since XP
- There are four CSEs provided by Microsoft that currently require synchronous foreground processing: Software Installation, Folder Redirection, Microsoft Disk Quota, and GP Preferences Drive Mapping
- **Avoid synchronous CSEs and *don't force synchronous policy*.**
- A WMI filter does not *automatically* slow down GP processing appreciably... *but*...
- If a WQL query implemented *in that filter* is time-consuming, it could slow down the startup or logon process.
- Costly WMI filters include those that rely heavily on network traffic, **such as LDAP queries**.
- Scripts running for a given user or computer, or scripts that hang or are no longer really in use, **can add to startup and logon times**.
- **Scripts that aren't responding will not timeout for 10 minutes, by default.**
- GP Preferences settings that use Item-Level Targeting (ILT) are not inherently harmful. However, certain kinds of Item Level Targeting queries can take more time to run.
- Costly ILT evaluations include all of the ILT types that must work over the network against AD to be evaluated: OU, **LDAP Query**, Domain, Site, and Computer Security Group filters.

Link: https://ctxpro.com/CHlinks/#34

Group Policy and AD References

James Rankin has some great thoughts about why you should make sure to enable asynchronous processing and NOT allow logon scripts to process synchronously:

Read up on GPP as well. Both links are at https://ctxpro.com/CHlinks/#35. My goal here is really to teach you the basics of what I find to work best.

Example

Here's our policy application diagram:

Baseline Policy
- Settings that apply universally to all
- OS Settings
- Security Baselines (for example, how clipboard and device attachments work)
- User Experience Baselines
- Folder Redirection and Profile Baseline settings

Delivery Exceptions
- Settings that apply specific to a Delivery Group or common Groups, often datacenter specific
- VDA Registration
- User Profile Management Paths
- Delivery-Group Specific UPM Exceptions or Additions
- Use Case Specific Delivery settings

User Exceptions
- Settings that are filtered by a specific AD User Group
- Security Poliices granting permissions
- Security denials
- User experience exceptions
- Office 365 exceptions

Citrix Policy Context Exceptions
- LAN Baseline
- WAN Exceptions
- Filtered by Subnet
- Filtered by Access Gateway

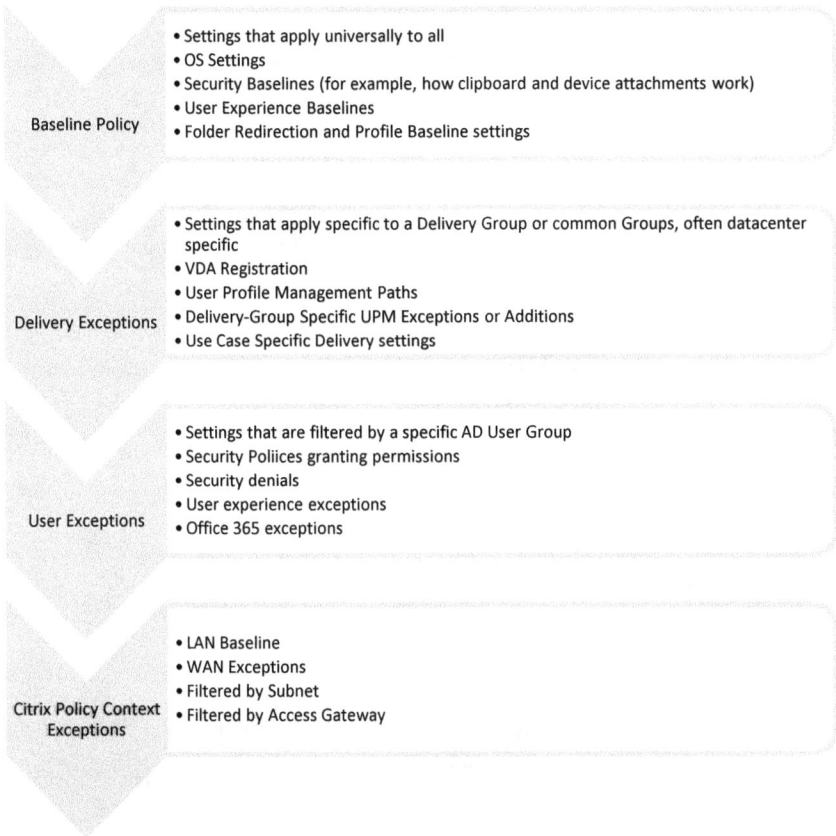

Figure 19: Policy Application (Plinko)

Let's say an environment has the following considerations:
- Windows 10 Non-Persistent VDAs with Office installed on Nutanix locally and Azure for Developers and Coders
- Windows 10 Persistent apps for development and IT
- Accounting Apps on Server OS published apps from PVS
- Office 365 for all users, but only the HR and Admin departments allow OST and PST files
- Acrobat Reader and Chrome on the Windows 10 VDIs
- Production Workflows are indicated by
  - 1 = Build or Maintenance machines
  - 2 = Test machines
  - 3 = Production machines

For this use case, we may see a GPO structure like this:

Domain
- Citrix Control
- Citrix Resource
  - o 1- Maintenance VMs
- Windows 10
- Production Desktop
  - o 2- Nutanix MCS TEST
  - o 3- Nutanix MCS PROD
  - o 3- Persistent
- Development Desktop
  - o 2- Azure MCS TEST
  - o 3- Azure MCS PROD
- Server 2016
  - o 2- Accounting Apps PVS TEST
  - o 3- Accounting Apps PVS PROD
  - o 2- PROD Apps PVS TEST
  - o 3- PROD Apps PVS PROD
- Citrix Groups

Let's then focus on the Resource OUs (the policy settings under each are in italics)

Citrix Resource
Citrix Baseline – settings common to everything such as in our case VDA registration
Security Baselines
User Drive Mapping (GPP) and Folder Redirection Policy
Clipboard and Local Drives Allowed – Policy applied to a specific user group allowing clipboard and attached drives
- **1- Maintenance VMs** (All Inheritance blocked)
  - *Maintenance Policy – starts Windows Update, allows Defrag, BIS-F rules*
- **Windows 10**

Windows 10 Baselines – common Desktop settings such as Internet Explorer, Adobe, Chrome and User Profile Management Rules for Windows 10

- o **Production Desktop**

  Nutanix MCS (assume copies of policies for test and prod)

  Nutanix MCS UPM Path – path specific to Windows 10 Nutanix VMs

  Outlook OST Allowed– applied only to user groups allowed to store OSTs. Includes GPP rules to create folders at logon if they don't exist

- o **Persistent**

  No Profile Management – Explicit turns off UPM processing

- o **Development Desktop**

  - ▪ Azure MCS

    Azure MCS UPM Path

- ● **Server 2016**

  Baseline – Sets RDSH Rules and User Profile Management Settings specific to 2016

  - o **Accounting Apps PVS**

    Accounting Apps UPM Path

  - o **PROD Apps PVS**

    PROD Apps UPM Path

Other Considerations

Resource Domains

One thing becoming more common (thankfully) is the use of entirely separate (either trusted or federated) domains for Control and Resources. While more work administratively, it has several advantages over a flat domain structure

- ● Fewer AD Objects to manage makes for faster AD performance
- ● No user accounts to manage serves to heighten security for the resource domain
- ● More granular administrative control
- ● One way trusts assure that even a compromised Resource domain would have no access to the primary user domain

- In multi-datacenter environments without resources in all datacenters, not having the resource domains synchronized to other datacenters lowers administrative overhead and security concerns
- My personal favorite: No possibility of policies intended for Citrix use cases being altered or overridden by User policies that can harm the environment

Of course, there are additional concerns about needing additional controllers, networking and licensing, backups, et cetera. I see more and more companies wisely adopt this 'trust but verify' structure made possible by using resource domains

Federated Domains

In my "quick wins" philosophy in this book, it is not feasible to fully cover the use of SAML for the federation of domains, but the concept is fantastic. Citrix has a service that overcomes a long-time limitation of doing federation in that an interactive Windows logon requires a token be passed. SAML alone cannot do this. However, the Citrix Federation Authentication Service (FAS) *can* accomplish this by using SAML to associate an external logon to an internal logon, then generating a virtual Smart Card token that is passed to the Windows logon service. This single-use token method has long been used with physical Smart Cards in government agencies for either direct logon or as a second factor identity. By passing a virtual authentication, the user is never even aware of what their actual logon name or password is on the resource domain. Further, because there is no domain trust relationship involved, unauthorized access is much more challenging to obtain. Finally, you can even opt to remove the logon process from your organization almost entirely by using federation services such as Okta with multi-factor authentication and/or One Time Passwords.

Workspace Environment Management

Another way to improve user experience and reduce reliance on the aging Active Directory infrastructure is to directly manage the workspace policies. Citrix acquired the French company Norksale a few years ago and makes the Workspace Environment Management (WEM) product available for those with a current subscription & license level. WEM has a lot of capabilities that are easy to use and some that are not quite as easily tapped.

For starters, WEM can manage many security and experience settings typically set by GPO or GPP, but do so at a 'smarter' point during the logon process, and even apply policy after the logon has occurred. Application whitelisting/blacklisting is possible as well as the application of user registry settings (remember, GPOs are just applying registry settings). But the strength of WEM is in resource controls such as CPU throttling and priority management as well as Memory trimming tools that can be crucial to our modern workspace that depends so greatly on tabbed browser sessions.

The primary advantage of WEM, however, is that it is able to apply settings dynamically, not having to rely on GPO Refresh or scripts to be run. So, we see a different dynamic in terms of our policy application matrix. There is more to say in the next chapter about WEM. In terms of policy application – our order of processing for the full stack looks like this:

Figure 20: Poilcy Application With WEM

Summary

As you can see, Active Directory design and policy application, in general, are make-or-break for the Citrix Engineer and very important for the Citrix Administrator to understand. My primary encouragement to you is to never stop learning in this regard. I'll be honest- in putting this chapter together I was reminded of some things I'd forgotten and even learned something new about the way Group Policy Preferences work!

The long and short of it is this: Active Directory management may have been around for a long time, but that by no means indicates you should sit back and think you know what you need to know. Remember: ASSUMPTION IS THE MOST DANGEROUS NEGATIVE FORCE IN All OF INFORMATION TECHNOLOGY.

Chapter 6: Quick Wins with WEM

Layers	• **Resource** • **Control**
Success Lanes	• Design • Build • Maintain
Prerequisites	• Windows Desktop and Server OS Knowledge • Windows Process Management Process • Registry and Group Policy Preferences, Logon Script impacts
Importance	🎸 🎸 🎸
User Impact	🎸 🎸 🎸 🎸 🎸
Security Impact	🎸 🎸 🎸 🎸
Difficulty	🎸 🎸 🎸

Don't Forget Your ABC's

A few years ago, Citrix purchased a company that I was, and I'll be honest, a little confused by at first. That is until I realized I'd forgotten my ABC's – *Always Blame Citrix*. I'm reasonably confident anyone that has been reading to this point has experienced the effect:

"Citrix   is   slow"
"Citrix   sucks"
"I   don't   want   to   run   Citrix..."

Possibly to provide a solution to the real problems that, in point of fact, rarely have ANYTHING to do with Citrix (as we know at this point hopefully), they acquired Norksale and in a move that surprised most of us veterans – made Workspace Environment Manager available to Advanced/Enterprise and above. In years past, acquisitions like this would tend to be a Platinum-only feature. The reason I include this in this new edition of the book comes down to another thing I started hearing in 2018 and started hearing more and more in 2019:

"When   can   I   get   onto   Citrix?"
"Oh my gosh, Citrix is so fast!"

That alone is good news. But the REALLY good news is how easy it is to have significant performance impacts, especially on Server OS, with WEM. I'll say right off the bat that one of the biggest things with Workspace Environment Manager is it's a pretty big tool, lots to do with it and a dedicated SQL infrastructure behind it. It may seem odd that I'm only pointing out some very simple things with such a powerful tool. Remember: what I'm after is impact with minimal effort. WEM was almost cut from my criteria for the Hero Project; until late 2018 when Google Chrome made a shift that severely impacted the amount of CPU and RAM consumed per tab.
What seemed like overnight, the world of performance in End User Computing (EUC) changed. While I agree with the security reasons behind the changes Chromium made, user experience suffered when memory resources became strained, and all the advantages of running Server OS seemed to evaporate.
One group of people were not having the issue; those that had already adopted and deployed WEM. Here's the excellent news: The highest impacts just happen to be some of the easiest to deploy.
Low effort, more hero.
I like it.

I want to highlight for you some of the things that you can do right away that will give you immediate results. You can take simple actions to get good results and avoid the law of diminishing returns (more on that in the next chapter) where we see that our definite impact increases, but our efforts decrease. We don't want increasing efforts with decreasing returns!

What is WEM or Workspace Environment Management?

Like other End User or Workspace Environment Managers, WEM uses system processes and/or an agent to make changes 'on the fly' to the programs and configuration for the user. Group Policy cannot do this without the user logging off or in some cases the entire machine rebooting.

WEM can directly influence program threads, lockdown, whitelist processes, and perform nearly any task involving the HKEY Local User. These would traditionally be done with Group Policy Preferences, but WEM can do them with context triggers in mind (as in, for example, how the environment should be treated if a user logs into a desktop from a different location). WEM is fantastic for deploying printers, managing aspects of security, and more.

In this chapter, I am going to focus on what I believe are the highest impacts for the least amount of effort. WEM is a complex tool that entire books could be written about in and of itself. We'll just focus on what will have the best impacts for your users, hero.

Why WEM?

An attractive reason to spend the small effort to deploy is the payoff in terms of how it can literally pay for itself. WEM can dramatically reduce the number of virtual machines that are required for serving a user workload. The net effect of that is also that you're getting more users per physical host, which is something that if you recall in chapters 1 and mostly in chapter 3, this saves money, which is often the biggest win of all.

Consider this scenario: 2012 R2 or 2016 Servers should *theoretically* be able to handle upwards of 100-200 users effectively with enough resources, but they're only getting about maybe 10 or less users on that machine (note, 2019 numbers haven't solidified quite yet). This is often because the applications that are installed there just aren't allowing for that kind of scalability to happen as they consume resources as if they had the processor and RAM all to themselves. Like small children that don't know any better – they don't realize they need to share.

This shouldn't be a shock to you. Most programs are developed to be deployed on a single PC. Concerns about resource "spending" don't factor into the developer's mandate in most cases. In a world of Minimum

Viable Product and increasingly powerful machines to handle them – rarely is performance a concern. Unfortunately, in an EUC environment, there isn't much that can be done, and we must find ways to work to make the programs themselves behave.

Resource Needs in EUC

In our example above, Chrome is a big memory hog, especially if you're like me, and you continuously have seven or eight thousand tabs open at any given time. It sucks down your memory pretty fast. I wrote this on a machine with 32 GB RAM on a regular basis, and very often, my RAM consumed is upwards of 70% on a day-to-day basis. If you put that into a VDI context, very rarely do I see a VM with over 8 GB RAM. I more commonly see 4 GB or less. The typical result is a slowdown as constant I/O happens with memory paging.

CPU can be a similar concern, not only with poorly programmed browser pages or apps but, at times, routine operations. If you have ever had to 'silo' a server because you have power users on Excel that are taking the system to a near halt for everyone else, you know to what I'm referring. While being on a hypervisor can help balance this overall – the reality is that unless the CPU is being consumed all day long, you typically have more servers you are maintaining exclusively to deal with this issue, or are using Desktop OS in a case that would otherwise not need it.

Securing Desktop Settings Based on Context

There are a lot of other desktop settings that are geared toward fine-tuning the user environment that are valuable, many of which you normally would do in Group Policy or Preferences. The common problem here is when you have to do settings for one group of users that differ from another. Very often, this creates even more silos – additional Delivery Groups with different GPOs applied.

Why different OUs? Remember, context filtering features of Group Policy Preferences will force processing to happen slower. The significant winning feature for many environments would be the ability to configure based not just on user membership, but a context that GPP can't process! Context such as, where the user is logging in from, all without having to maintain silos to do it.

Optimizing and Reducing Logon Scripts

There are more complicated things you can do to win with WEM, such as whitelisting and blacklisting programs & executables directly, a great security play with the agent already running. Also, generally speaking, a way to reduce the amount of resources that are taking up on a machine you can banish certain applications from running that really increase the number of users you can get on every server.

Eliminating logon scripts by adding those functions being done into WEM instead can also help logon times. Logon scripts are one of the last remaining bastions of bad practices that are out there today as we've discussed. The vast majority of things that I see for logon scripts that make any sense are things that you can do instead via WEM.

Learning to Share (Resources)

There are some caveats, but generally speaking, the significant impact is on Multi-Session OS: more users on fewer servers (meaning both virtual machines and actual physical hosts.)

Case Study

I am using some examples from an actual case study here - even just a small little environment of 250 users (that, by the way, grew to nearly 400 using the same hardware after what we did there). We implemented the settings you're going to see here.

*Thanks to these settings, we demonstrated at one point that we could run everything off of **three servers**. I don't recommend pushing to extremes like that unless you need to, but in our particular case, we found that users that were once complaining about performance at 12 servers now running on three with no complaints. This wasn't on purpose, of course – an accident by an admin. But I hope this sinks in: They had the full workload on those three servers and nobody said a word. That gives you an idea about how well Workspace Environment Management works in these scenarios. Your results might vary, but generally speaking, I'm finding everywhere I put WEM in, there are benefits across the board.*

As far as that goes for quick wins: scalability and speed are the most visible things that make you the Citrix Hero. The good news is that these are the easiest effects to start getting in under an hour by deploying WEM. That's pretty cool. Sales pitch over. Let's get into it.

Quick Wins with System Optimizations

Remember- significant benefits with minimal effort is what we're after here. I recommend emulating settings that work at a baseline first and then fine-tuning as you get more experienced with the product.

There are some great videos out there from people like Hal Lange [https://ctxpro.com/CHlinks/#36] that show you how this all works. Because I feel video is possibly the best venue, I also make the video teaching of this chapter available to you with your book purchase at https://ctxpro.com/herobonus7 along with links to other resources I try to keep up to date.

CPU Management

A goal of CPU management is to control individual programs' usage of the CPU in ways that balance usability with "staying in your lane" and not having said program encroach on others inappropriately. The way this works in WEM is much more intelligent than some of the traditional ways that used to be done (Microsoft and Citrix previously had 'fair sharing' methods that pretty much clamp a programs' overall performance rather than adjusting it appropriately).

CPU Spikes Protection

Spikes protection works by setting a percentage of overall CPU during a sample time and determining when that process is using too much. If it's using past a specific limit, WEM can throttle down to that percentage of utilization until the processing is done. In a Server OS (don't make me say it... XenApp...) VDA, this is very useful to make sure that a heavy process that may be intended for background processing or just badly coded doesn't affect everyone else on that system. This setting is sometimes instrumental in VDI environments where the CPU on the host is being overrun, and you want to limit that along with overall priority controls.

103

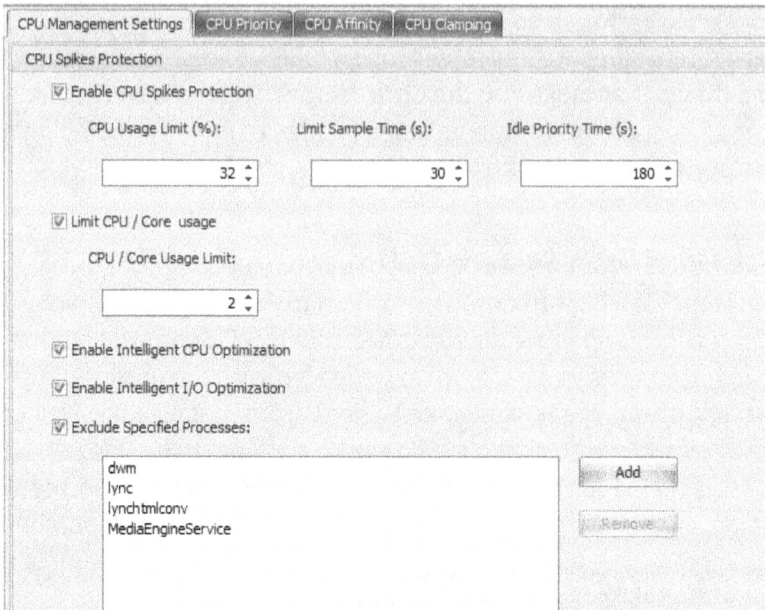

Figure 21: CPU Management Settings in WEM 7.15

The limit value seems on the surface as if it would restrict a process to a certain amount of utilization. However, this is not the case. "Limit" is a trigger that tells the optimization to begin after the threshold has been exceeded.

On a system where you want to limit a process to trigger optimization after it exceeds what a single vCPU would typically allow, CPU Spikes Protection limits are best determined by dividing 100% by the number of cores, then down 1%. For a 4 vCPU server you'd set spike protection to 24%. For 3 vCPU, 32% et cetera. Note that this is not a requirement, but it is where I tend to start!

Another aspect that you may want to play around with is the Limit Sample Time, which sets how often a process is sampled for its percentage to determine if it's reached a limit that needs to be reduced.
You can also set a limit on the number of CPU cores that can be used – a setting that I rarely see any demonstrable impact in having. In theory, this can be used with or without the limits set.

Intelligent CPU Optimization is my favorite setting here, and what tends to make the most positive impact. If a process has 'violated' the usage limit threshold too many times in a session, this setting will automatically reduce the process priority for the duration of the session so that even if the CPU spike happens, it will be at a lower CPU priority.

I have seen spikes protection work very well in VDI in accounting scenarios where the user wants to start an analysis process but continue working in the foreground… but the program is poorly coded to use 100% CPU even if it doesn't need it to function. Yes, it really does happen, and that is something processes are allowed to do. WEM helps keep that lazy programming in check!

An important note here is to exclude some critical processes from Spikes Protection & Optimization. Of particular note here are programs like Skype/Lync and the ICA MediaEngine that can be detrimental to the user experience if they have limits. Make sure that a program is well-coded before you exclude it from Spikes protection!

CPU Priority

Another very powerful setting in WEM is the ability to specify when programs can be allowed to use full or limited use of the processor on a schedule defined by priority. This function of nearly every operating system that exists today is what allows multitasking to occur effectively.

Not to get too deep into this, but to understand why this is a quick and easy win – let's say that a modern OS uses a scheduler to determine at each clock cycle of a CPU what is completed first and what should wait for the next available cycle. Windows has several levels (Linux can have even more), but the most important to us will be Above Normal, Normal, Below Normal, and Idle.

Most processes in a system run at Normal, meaning they will share evenly with each other. The problem in an EUC environment (Server OS especially) is that the sheer number of running processes can cause the CPU Scheduler to treat processes that don't add immediate value the same as those that do.

For example, while Microsoft Outlook benefits the user by performing well in most cases – it also uses a lot of background processes that don't always provide direct benefit. If executed at a normal priority, other programs may have to wait for these processes to complete before they are given enough cycles to complete the process. By asking Outlook to wait for these background processes by setting the priority to Below Normal, it uses any cycles not already spoken for at that level or above it. In the three years I've been using WEM in production environments, I have never had this cause an issue. I *have,* however, had users complement how much more 'peppy' the system is, and system admins comment that they can get more users per VM when this was enabled.

Let us say that a process can be run in the background entirely without negative impacts.

We can run a process like this at Below Normal or Idle. I will very often use this method for programs like browsers where they tend to be a little 'power-mad,' but the user does not notice a difference if made to wait.

Certain programs that rely on immediate results with no interruption in cycles, in contrast, tend to cause user complaints if left as Normal. Skype (Lync.exe) is an excellent example of this at scale. The process needed to be Above Normal so that nothing else could take the priority away from that and it behaves well enough that you can do so without taking over the system. You never need to know about your aggregate user experience at that point (for example, if it is just used for chat it may not need the power – audio and video are a different story). For those kinds of real-time communications, you typically want that to be Above Normal, so you combine that with the spikes protection and the optimization in general and it tends to work very well.

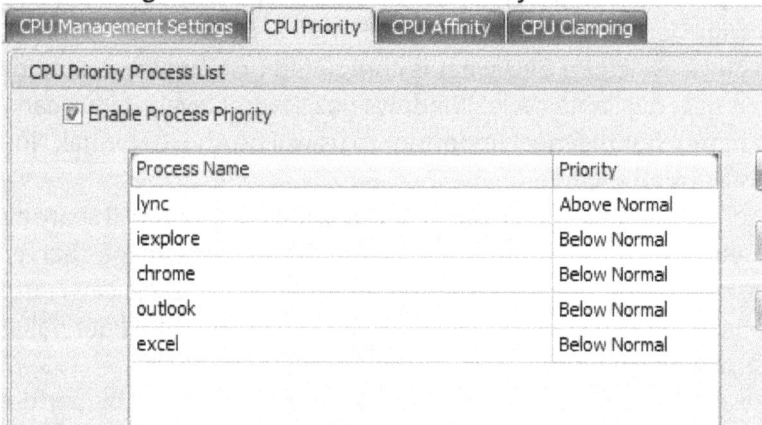

Figure 22: CPU Priority in WEM

Another way to look at CPU priority is if you have an inbox full of items vs. a desk with scattered papers all over it. What is at the top of my inbox is my *first* priority on which to work. When I accomplish that, I work down the other bins. Having a priority rather than dividing my time ends up being more effective.

I'm going to break the fourth wall here a little and say that writing this book is the perfect example here. I wanted to publish this book in the fall of 2019. Here I am typing this March 1st, 2020. Why? Because I worked on other things and attempted to multi-task. The reality is, tragically, that I have very little to show in terms of progress for my multi-tasking. It wasn't until I decided to make this project a priority that it got done. And when I say a priority, I mean that in a single week I decided to spend the first 4 hours of each day working on this. Two weeks later, and it is finished. I had other work to perform during that time. And you know what? The work still got done. Setting the priority for what I did first in my day, worked to get the task done. I guess what I'm in effect saying is that I need WEM for my professional life as much as you need WEM for your Citrix environment.

If everything set to "Normal" then nothing is.

Normal is 'fair' when it isn't always fair. Whatever gets there first or is next in line. This does not lend itself to ideal performance in life and doesn't in computing either.
As with anything – don't just take my word for it. Test with your users and get feedback!
A quick note on this. If you are properly managing the CPU Priority, **do not fear 100% Utilization!** Videos exist demonstrating this, and I have tested this myself: even running at 100% CPU, a system can still be responsive and effective when WEM is managing the CPU!

When a CPU uses a better scheduler to execute things more effectively, it thrives. If you have poorly behaving programs at Below Normal, the other programs that are more crucial do their work faster, releasing the cycles for other work to be done. You end up in most cases that I've seen with higher CPU utilization reported by the OS and Hypervisor. Don't be afraid of that! It might take some staff training to undo years and years of hearing that "high CPU utilization equals bad experience for users," but with WEM, that changes. Put it to the test!

Back to the story of having 12 servers down to three by accident and nobody knew the difference. The main thing we noticed is that those virtual machines were running at 100% processor the entire time; yet the user experience was completely normal.

Note here, when it comes to monitoring, if you're running WEM properly on those servers, your monitoring should only be focused on the user experience itself. For example, CPU usage is not a good indicator of EUC performance, but user input delay *is* a good indicator of trouble. Latency, especially response latency in ICA, is another indicator of trouble that is more highly valuable than CPU or even Memory usage when properly optimizing with WEM!

CPU Clamping

Another setting that I don't recommend often, but I have used to prove a point, is CPU Clamping which completely locks down a process from the moment it is launched to a certain usage limit.

I won't get myself in trouble by mentioning the exact product, but my team and I conducted a test on this in late 2018. We found the program performed the same way if it was clamped or if it was using 100% CPU! There's no real benefit to them doing so. What we found was that there was no difference in the execution times between having a limit or no limit. An occasional challenge with legacy programs is that they attempt to 'lock' 100% of whatever threads it can find. Interestingly enough, this doesn't always mean it won't release the threads, just that you observe an entirely locked CPU core, as an example.

I have occasionally set Clamping in combination with CPU Priority rules on certain malware and antivirus programs that become the villain instead of the hero. Far better to leave them running, of course, just limiting their environmental impact than disabling them completely!

Note- Unless you have a lot of these programs that cycle up and down more frequently than a realistic sample time can be set, I still recommend *CPU Spikes Protection over CPU Clamping.* This helps you prevent that condition from occurring but an intelligent way where it's doing it based on if you'd been on for too long.

Memory Management

The other winning feature with Workspace Environment Manager is Memory Management. There are no complicated things to do here; just check the box! Let it run, test it out, and see how it does! Optimization dramatically reduces the bottlenecks to getting more people to be able to work on a single operating system by releasing active RAM and more intelligently using Windows Memory Manager.

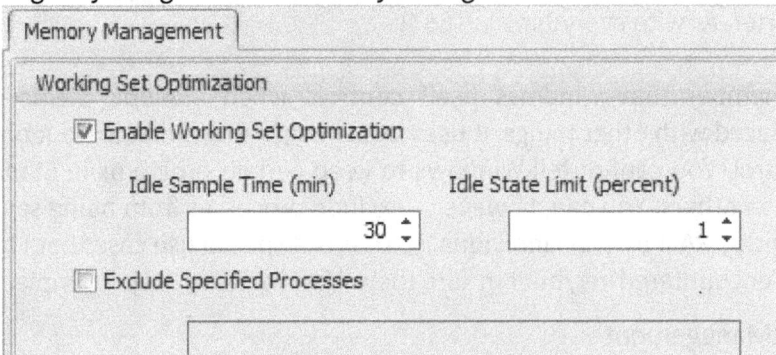

Figure 23: Memory Management Settings

Remember that Windows wasn't built from the ground up to house multiple users on a system, and the way it uses memory by default reflects that. The problem with consuming too much memory is that you start to use the page file, which causes a pausing effect in your sessions. Sometimes CPU is blamed when the problem is memory-related.

What Working Set Optimization does is take memory pages that haven't been used for a long time and put them into a lower priority state in memory. In EUC, Chrome is a big offender when each user has lots of tabs open. Every single one of those is a dedicated process and lives in its own memory space. Having 20 open tabs seems to be the new human condition. I get to the end of my workday and often find even more than that open. Yet- I haven't touched the tab in hours. It is just sitting there consuming RAM.

What WEM essentially does is to instruct Windows to move those active pages into standby RAM. Standby RAM is available until something else replaces it (flushing it to the paging file). In terms of performance, if a bit of memory hasn't been read or written in quite some time, the odds are good it won't be needed again very quickly, if at all. This holds true with browser tabs. There is probably not going to be any impact in having to

109

re-load into working set memory from the page file – but you have the option. Further, even loading back from the paging file doesn't matter to the user experience – in many cases it feels as normal as a page refreshing itself. In other words – your user rarely notices.

All that said, mind your sample time! In some Single-Session VDI cases, this should be set longer. In some Multi-Session OS Desktops, it should be shorter. As with everything... TEST!

Remember that Windows itself controls when standby memory is replaced with other things. It uses its own algorithms that are out of our control. You cannot tell Windows to keep certain programs in Standby above others. You can, however – exclude processes from being sent to Standby RAM by WEM individually. That is a special use case that I have not encountered yet, but I'm sure they exist. For now, keep it simple!

I/O Management

WEM can also influence the overall priority of when a process requests disk Input and Output. This is NOT to say IO per second (IOPS) decreases. Much like CPU management, you are scheduling processes more appropriately. In fact, you may see *more* IOPS – but that increase may indicate improved user experience!

Like CPU Management, you have priorities such as High, Normal, Low, and Very Low. WEM instructs Windows to override what the program is requesting. For example, "Trusted Installer" occasionally runs even in a non-persistent VDA where it has little value to the user experience – yet it can't be disabled safely. The same goes for when you have updates that are trying to run, or you have processes from SCCM are doing a scan of the environment for auditing and don't add any value to the user experience. You're telling Windows to do those tasks when it can; that it doesn't have to be right away. If another process needs the IO, Windows tells the others to wait while it fulfills that request.

Process Name	I/O Priority
trustedinstaller	Low
msseces	Low

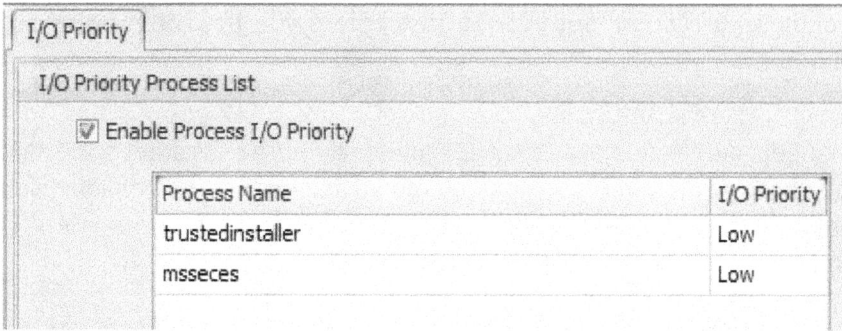

Figure 24: Settings for IO Priority in WEM

In our example, Chrome can be I/O intensive for not very good reasons. From a system perspective, we have other things that are more important for us, and we set those processes to be a higher priority.

In another field example, the client had QuickBooks running on Multi-Session OS VDAs. We don't care that the Update Manager wants disk IO, but we need it to at least be running because of a program requirement. Windows doesn't know this on its own. We are telling it what is important to us and what is not in terms of time and experience.

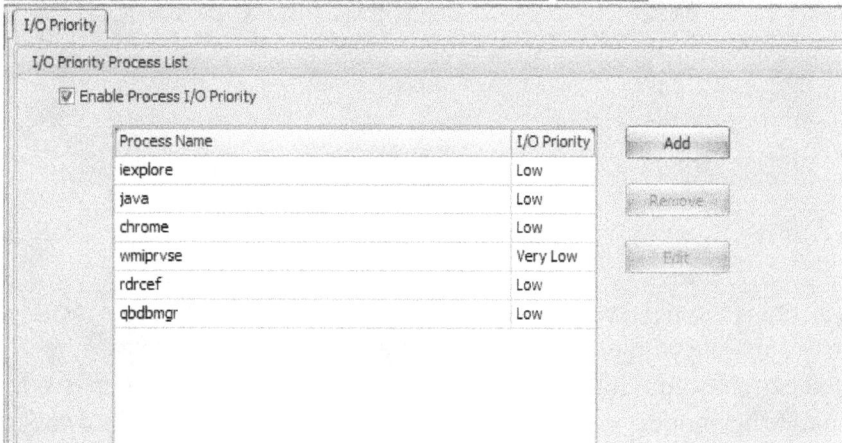

Process Name	I/O Priority
iexplore	Low
java	Low
chrome	Low
wmiprvse	Very Low
rdrcef	Low
qbdbmgr	Low

Figure 25: A Field Example of IO Priority Settings

Policies and Profiles Settings

There are a significant number of settings in the Policies and Profiles section. Entire books could be written about these settings. Remember that I want to focus on the lower effort items that will give the most impact. I have decided to give you a few examples of how I will typically

BE A CITRIX HERO

configure a system, but PLEASE test before you put these items into production.

Environmental Settings

Our goal here is to make the user experience more consistent and SAFER by enacting certain restrictions. Some advice here as well, making sure that IT Administrators are not included in any of these restrictions is often important for the sake of troubleshooting.

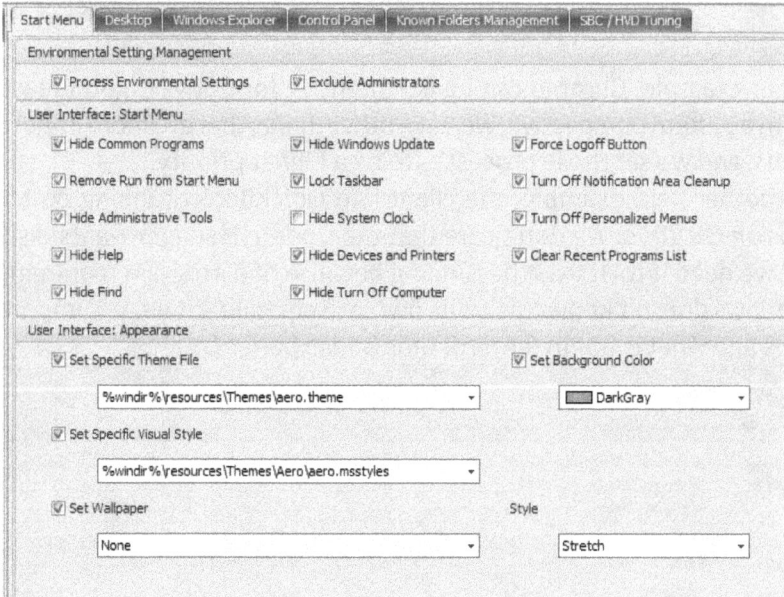

Figure 26: WEM Environmental Settings Example – Start Menu

You may notice right away that most of these settings are often included in Group Policy Objects – so why not manage them there?

You certainly could! But I find this not only easier but also keep in mind that if the Agent is running, you can apply these changes right away for users and apply context that GPO can't. For quick & easy wins – this is, in my opinion, way easier than trying to find these GPO settings. Some of these settings are aesthetic, and some don't even matter anymore. Most settings, however, are to keep the user safe from their inexperience or bad practices like saving things to the C drive on a non-persistent VM.

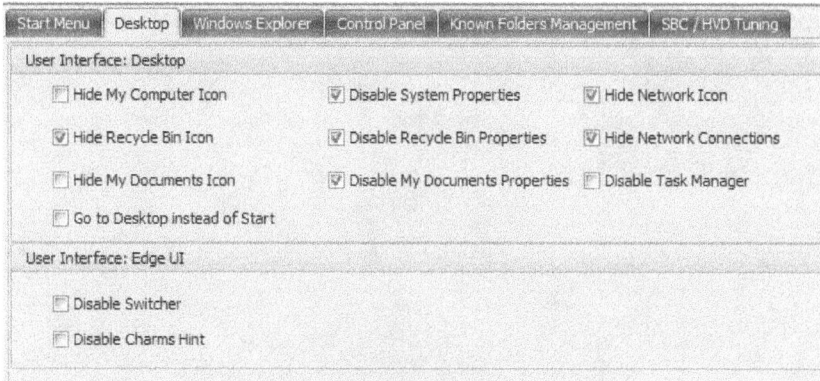

Figure 27: Desktop Settings Example

These are some pretty easy ways to get some quick wins as far as controlling the user experience. Keep in mind, there are certain things that users themselves probably don't even realize they have access to, but if they are running a program that does and it's running on their behalf, *they have access.* WEM helps keep this from happening.

This helps with security as a whole, but I also find that restricting drives and hiding drives reduces risks from more than a security sense. Again, this is something you can do in group policy, but WEM is a lot easier of an interface with which to work.

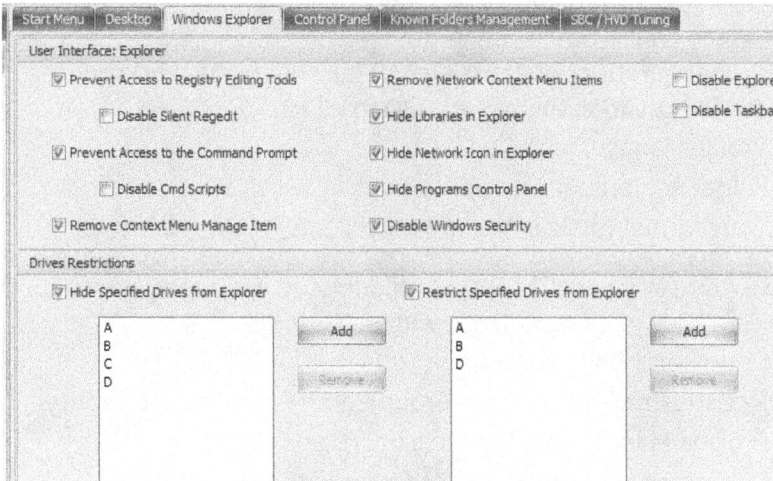

Figure 28: Windows Explorer Settings Example

113

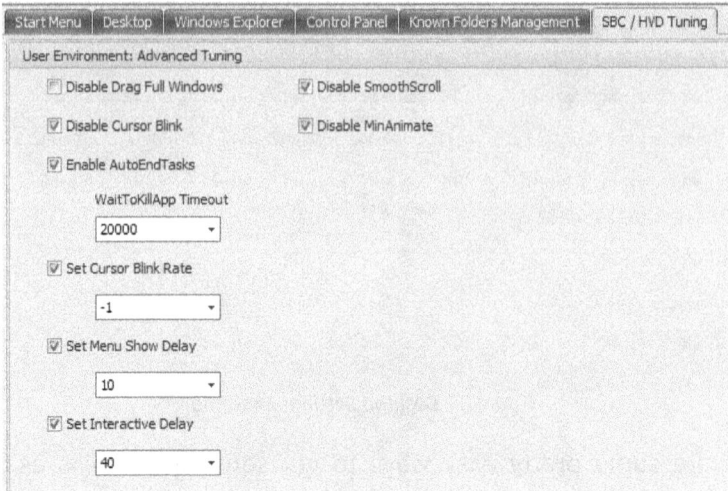

Figure 29: Tuning Settings Example

I also fully realize that screenshots rarely work to convey instructions – so I recommend loading the default templates that come with WEM and fine-tuning as you need to. Also, remember to view the included lesson online for this chapter as I go into a lot more detail.

Items NOT to Configure (yet)

There are a few things that I recommend waiting on when it comes to Workspace Environment Management; if you are adding it into a system that already has been configured.

These configurations are possible but may not be beneficial vs. the effort needed to transition them from GPO to WEM:

- Profile Management
- Folder Redirection
- Transformer (makes PCs into thin clients)

These items are beneficial, but I recommend waiting to transition them until you have good experience with WEM:

- Printer and Drive Mapping
- Registry Entries (replacing Group Policy Preferences or Policy)
- Process Management (Whitelisting/Blacklisting)
- Publishing StoreFront-sourced apps in the Start Menu

If you have a new environment and you want to run it because you are comfortable, I'm supportive of this idea. However, as far as transferring these functions from where they are into WEM, I don't find there's enough benefit to justify the learning curve and to do it down the road.

There is much power in replacing logon scripts, drive mappings, and more with WEM. But until the entire team is comfortable – I recommend waiting on these functions.

I have one client that has no idea how to do anything with WEM. It manages performance, and that's perfectly okay for them. They don't have any problems that I need to ever change anything. We spent about five hours of effort. That was about two years ago, and everything's been fine since. These wins are quick, and they stay put for a long time.

If you *are* installing net-new, however – I would absolutely deploy these policies with WEM first!

Finally, I will say that WEM is probably one of the more complex software Citrix has with shockingly little documentation as of this writing.

I thought I'd share some of the bookmarks I keep in my browser and hope that they stick around for years to come! [https://ctxpro.com/CHlinks/#37]

BONUS CHAPTER – Change Management

"Laddie, you've got a lot to learn if you want people to think of you as a miracle worker!"
-Montgomery Scott (fictional)

I wish that my career was filled with rosy pictures of perfect projects. However, the reality is this: I've spent more time as a consultant called into the midst of calamities. Calamites that could have been avoided had better change management been followed.

Key Concepts

A far too frequently overlooked aspect of being a hero is that a hero does not act carelessly or in a way that harms those they are trying to serve and protect. Yet, time and again, I find that one of the largest areas of risk in IT departments has little to do with what technology is being deployed or the configurations being deployed themselves. It has everything to do with *how the technology is being managed.*

Let me say right away that I made MANY mistakes over the years because frankly, no one told me how to manage IT projects. I was "The IT Guy" and was winging it for easily the first decade of my IT career. Now, as I conduct more and more assessments, I find the problem is not just limited to people. IT is very often its own worst enemy because of the way they deploy. Citrix is a USER-CENTRIC technology, and it is crucial to be deliberate and purposeful about how you deploy changes.

Unfortunately, there's no such thing as an industry-standard in change control (though certainly some popular methods at this point!) There are a lot of methodologies and procedures that may be followed in your organization; at least, I hope. The problem, especially in a crisis, is that the rules are often bypassed. Why? Because this needs to be something you believe in first and follow as procedure second.

To illustrate what I mean, I will start with a story of some deployments I have been either part of or involved in... well, the cleanup. I'll give an example of how it, unfortunately, went with one deployment, and then I'll demonstrate a better way to go about it using my riskLESS Methodology. As you can imagine, the names have been omitted, and a couple of small details changed here and there to make sure that we're not embarrassing anyone.

The Bad Project

The first example is a very common scenario of a company with XenApp 6/5 on Server 2008 R2. They were upgrading to Citrix XenDesktop 7.15 LTSR and upgrading their control servers to Server 2016. In addition, they were also doing a hypervisor upgrade and throwing a storage upgrade in the mix!

Because, why not, right?

I witnessed this scenario play out four times in 2019 alone, and I cringed each time. But I'm jumping ahead. Suffice it to say, this is a common scenario with the End of Life of Windows Server 2008 R2 having passed and support ending for XenApp 6.5 as well.

The team looked at the work involved and assumed they could do the upgrade within a week. Not an unreasonable assumption based on the amount of actual deployment work involved. At least, that was the expectation when management asked them how long it would take to do the upgrade.

Project Kickoff

They met with the vendor and "looked at what was going on" and theorized what should be done. They had a new Server Administrator that had been "VolunTold" into "doing the Citrix thing" that has been running for a long time in the background with no one truly familiar with it.

They found rather quickly that there wasn't enough time given the week-long timeline to do any practical testing for issues. Their thought was, "simply" upgrade the servers in place from 2008 R2 to 2016.

Deployment

As you may imagine, they found right away five applications that would not run or install on Server 2016. Because they weren't prepared for this, they decided to migrate the 2008 R2 VMs to the new site and install the new VDA on those existing servers registering to the new environment. For the record, this was a supported procedure at the time and often not

117

a bad idea when you can fix applications later on in the process. Oh, if only it were that simple in these cases.

Midway into their process, they upgraded VMware (their hypervisor). Those of you experienced in such upgrades are probably already cringing. Just wait. It gets even better! They attached the new storage and moved all the servers onto it, created the new environments, and everything was looking like it was going to be an easy weekend of continuing the deployment with no issues.

The procedure is simple enough.
1. Uninstall the XenApp components.
2. Install the XenDesktop 7.15 components.
3. They even figure out that they can deploy machines using Machine Creation Services to save time and hassle later. Everything seems fine!

Everything was NOT fine

As you're probably guessing, everything was not fine. A storage issue occurred, but in an unfortunate twist of fate, they found that it's not possible to back this change out easily. While they could revert some things, they found that in their hurry, a critical backup had not been taken.

Monday comes, and everything in Citrix is down.

While it takes all day, they do manage to get the upgrade up and running. However, a few days later, they start to encounter more and more complaints about printing, Citrix "not working," and generally poor performance.

The service desk staff was being overwhelmed with calls. IT was busier than it ever had been chasing down issues that they didn't understand. It worked before, after all, so why wouldn't an upgrade make it even better? (for those of you who actually believe that is ever true, I have some beachfront property here in Nashville to sell you.)

Mitigation Attempts

Vendors suggest rolling things back, which is not an option in their case. They are stuck with what they have now and have to make it work.

However, it gets worse after a couple of days of chasing the issues. The CIO calls the entire IT department together in a high-stress meeting. In the course of this meeting, it was determined that the most important thing right now to resolve is the performance issues, so that's their focus. Of course, the CIO was not pleased because they couldn't just roll it back to the way it was. They're stuck with it now, and their phone is ringing non stop about the issues. Plans to move other things forward are being delayed because of this issue. Revenue is being impacted, which would typically send even the calmest CIO into a firing frenzy.

The newly appointed Citrix Administrator had been reading blog posts and suggested a change. Given how upset the CIO is and how management was coming down on them, they didn't want to wait. So, they made a change mid-day unannounced. It disrupts the system entirely for about three hours. Ouch.

Then they rolled that change back (fortunately, they could roll *that* back, having learned their lesson the previous week.)

That put them back to where they were three hours ago, but the problem is that at that point, it was clear that management had no confidence in them. Their now red-faced CIO ordered no more changes to be made. They're stuck with this poorly performing system, but they don't want their team to make any more changes.

Change Freeze

More meetings determine that the main issues are occurring in only one application, but the issue is still causing massive performance degradation across the board.

Finally, after a month of back-and-forth regarding what potential causes and fixes could be, management decides to hire outside Consulting Services. Unfortunately, it's not like the fire department where they come rushing in. Usually, there's a whole procurement process, especially if you're working with Citrix Consulting, many times there's a backlog of work being conducted even if the procurement process is accelerated.

Consulting Fixes It

And so, 180 days into the project, the consultants finally arrive and make some assessments. Within a week or so, they make some determinations as far as what actions to take.

They determined that there were additional hardware requirements to address the performance issues. In this case, they were fortunate and managed to get the new hardware in under three days, which is pretty rare (I typically see more like 3 months for getting new server hardware.) It brings performance up to the standards that they originally wanted.

119

Consulting fixes the other issues as well, and the company does end up with a higher-performing system than they had previously in the end. But unfortunately, the damage had already been done. The CIO was "asked" to step down, but not before they fired most of the IT staff and stopped doing business with the vendor that suggested the initial course of action.

It was a nightmare scenario, but an authentic example of precisely what my colleagues and I are seeing more and more frequently (yes, more, not less).

Summary

What bothers me about all this is that it is all preventable. That's why I wanted to go through this lesson and make sure that we as Citrix Heroes understand what these concepts are and how to prevent these "Resume Generating Opportunities." Because more often than not- it is these soft skills that matter even more than our technical knowledge!

More often than not- it is these soft skills that matter even more than our technical knowledge!

Methodology Matters

This is where we come back to my "RiskLESS" Services Methodology:
- Understand
- Plan
- Change
- Maintain

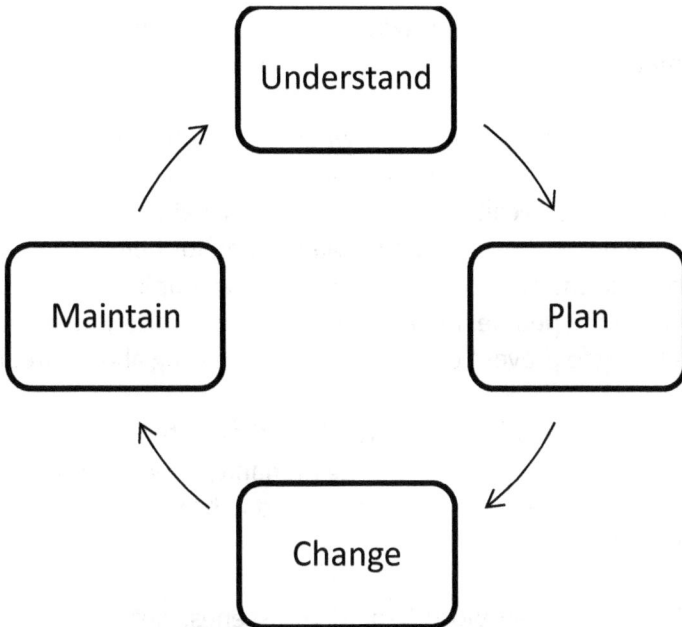

Figure 30: DJ's riskLESS Methodology

Can you see where this was NOT followed in the example I gave? They just kept moving forward with their Change instead of stopping and going back to Understand phase. Worse, they never validated their Plan (or ever had a solid Plan at all – they just deployed with no validation).

Thinking Proactively

To avoid these risks, **Heroes think proactively**. We don't "power through it"; jump into the Change and hope everything's going to be alright. We Plan, make a Test Change, come back to Understand with new information, adjust our Plan, Test again, and only when everything meets our goals, do we proceed to Change production.

Remember, Hero - you need to be the person that is shielding your users from risks, not causing harm! We can't say things like "Oh, well, it's not a big deal... Nobody died!"

There are scenarios in health care, for example, where people *have* actually died because they've been turned away from care because systems were down. Take this seriously!

You need to be someone who's not introducing things into the environment that cause harm where it should have been making things better.

Additionally, (and I'll admit this is where the Hero analogy falls apart a little bit) is that the hero needs to follow a process that prevents people from ever needing to call for help! This is not usually the comic book and movie storyline. The people are usually calling for help, not the heroes. Other times, in the case of The Avengers, for example, there was no call for help from the people. Instead, we had an organization called Shield that was trying to prevent people from ever knowing about threats.

Men in Black was another storyline where there's this secret thing going behind the scenes, proactively saving humanity in ways they never even knew. I'll be honest and say I always wanted to be wearing a cool suit and sunglasses all day.

I think in IT, we often work behind the scenes, not the big dramatic superhero; much more like another comic book group of heroes with no "superpowers," just dedication.

Either way, we do these sometimes-thankless jobs that most people don't even realize we are doing. They don't realize it because hopefully, we're doing so well that people don't even realize the risks they face. They've been… SHIELD-ded.

Better Change Management

Let's take another look at our scenario and rethink the way changes are made in the environment. Currently, the thinking doesn't go much beyond "There is a new need identified, so just make changes in production."

As we're moving to more of a Cloud-focused world where we have terms like DevOps and such, I see more desire to iterate changes more rapidly. As a result, I'm seeing more risks being taken that really shouldn't be taken.

I'm seeing more and more changes being made with the attitude that if it doesn't work, just roll it back.

The problem is that you've already violated that that first rule we talked about:

We've already done harm to the people.

Don't Expose Users to Risks

You should shield your users from being the first to experience changes, even if it means you have to do the changes on a slower kind of fashion (or slower rollout), or work behind the scenes more than 'just doing it' (forgive the pun I'm making here– my first book on IT Services Methodology is called Just Do THIS).

As an example, let's consider the typical three-phase process in PVS and MCS for maintaining vDisk images for single-image deployments. You have a Maintenance VM, then Test VMs, and finally, Production. This does a great deal to shield from many risks when it is used properly.

The conceptual standpoint is limiting exposure of risks to users.

1. First, we make some changes to our Maintenance VM that we think meets our needs.
2. Then we test those changes.
3. Only if those changes are determined to have either less or no risk while still meeting our objectives, do we roll them out for Production.
4. This means the people that are in production are never really exposed to those negative effects that could potentially be there as we've identified them in testing.

Risk Management in the Enterprise

If Citrix is considered "mission-critical," then a more granular approach is needed. For example, many of these environments have a kind of Sandbox environment – wholly isolated in many cases so that it doesn't even touch the production domain or, in some cases, even had dedicated hardware to allow for complete validation testing. Some environments will refer to this as "Test" or "Development (Dev)". I typically like "Development" more than "Test" for this level of isolation.

What I tend to see as a "Test" environment is one that is set aside for some networking isolation but ultimately is still connected to production Active Directory and services either directly or through a router. You're still talking to the production network; you're just doing so in a much less exposed fashion.

Sample from "Just Do THIS"

There's a lot more to say here, and since I've already written on the subject, I thought I'd give you a pre-edit sample of a chapter in my book "Just Do THIS" instead of re-writing it. Cheating, perhaps. But it's my

123

work. I can do what I want, right? (The book is scheduled for release in Summer of 2020 – visit MethodologyBook.com to learn more!)

TESTING IS THE MOST IMPORTANT AND MOST OVERLOOKED DIFFERENTIATOR BETWEEN COMPANIES THAT DESIRE RISK MANAGEMENT OVER 'JUST GETTING IT DONE.' IN MY EXPERIENCE, THOSE COMPANIES THAT IMPLEMENT MULTIPLE STAGES OF TESTING HAVE THE LEAST NUMBER OF NEGATIVE INCIDENTS.

AS MY FRIEND WHO WAS THE CTO OF A CHILDREN'S HOSPITAL SAID,

"IN SIX MONTHS, NO ONE WILL REMEMBER WHEN WE WENT LIVE. THEY WILL REMEMBER HOW WE WENT LIVE."

TESTING BEFORE A CHANGE GOES INTO PRODUCTION IS HOW YOU PREVENT A BAD PERCEPTION, KEEP MANAGEMENT HAPPY (WELL, HAPPIER THAN THEY WOULD BE OTHERWISE), AND GENERALLY AVOID THOSE LATE-NIGHT PHONE CALLS AND MISSED VACATIONS. BUT EQUALLY IMPORTANT TO THIS IS STRATEGICALLY ASSURING THAT USERS DO NOT HAVE A NEGATIVE PERCEPTION OF PROJECTS, AND MOST ASSUREDLY THAT MANAGEMENT DOES NOT SEE THE TESTING RESULTS OF A PROCESS TOO EARLY (WHICH COULD KILL PROGRESS PREMATURELY.)

TESTING METHODOLOGY

TESTING METHODOLOGY SHOULD INCLUDE A GRADUALLY INCREASING POPULATION EXPOSED TO THE PROPOSED CHANGE, TYPICALLY IN FOUR PRIMARY PHASES PLUS A PRODUCTION PILOT. EACH PHASE MAY NEED TO BE CANCELED AND RETURNED TO THE PREVIOUS PHASE WHEN CHANGES ARE REQUIRED. THIS ITERATIVE PROCESS, MUCH LIKE THE METHODOLOGY ITSELF, SHOULD BE VISUALIZED AS A CIRCULAR FLOW WHERE CHANGES ARE POSSIBLE RIGHT UP TO THE POINT OF PRODUCTION.

1. **DEVELOPMENT TESTING** (DEV/TEST). THE INFORMATION TECHNOLOGY PROFESSIONALS (TYPICALLY IN THIS CASE ENGINEERS) WILL TAKE THE DESIGN FROM THE ARCHITECTS AND PROVE FUNCTIONALITY IN A DEDICATED NON-PRODUCTION ENVIRONMENT. BY DEDICATED, I TYPICALLY MEAN JUST THAT - DEDICATED TO THAT FUNCTION. THE MOST SUCCESSFUL ISOLATIONS I SEE ARE TYPICALLY DEDICATED FROM THE HARDWARE LAYER TO THE USER AND ACCESS LAYERS. THIS MEANS THAT THEY HAVE DEDICATED COMPUTE AND STORAGE, DEDICATED ACTIVE DIRECTORY, DATABASES, EVERYTHING THAT IS

FEASIBLE. WHILE THIS IS NOT ALWAYS POSSIBLE AND YOU SHOULD ALWAYS CHECK WITH VENDORS; MOST WILL HAPPILY ACCOMMODATE LICENSING FOR NON-PRODUCTION USE IN THIS REGARD. BUT REMEMBER - YOUR AUDIENCE HERE IS 100% INFORMATION TECHNOLOGY TEAMS. THE ODDS OF FAILURE ARE MUCH HIGHER SO CONTROLLING PERCEPTIONS ABOUT THE PROJECT IS CRUCIAL. THE OTHER PERSPECTIVE TO HAVE HERE IS THAT THIS MUST BE THE MOST AGILE ENVIRONMENT. YOU MUST BE ABLE TO MAKE SMALL ADJUSTMENTS IMMEDIATELY WITH ONLY HAVING TO INFORM A SMALL NUMBER OF PEOPLE.

2. **VALIDATION TESTING**. MANY CHANGES CAN IMPACT SYSTEMS IN WAYS THAT THE IT TEAM CANNOT ALWAYS ANTICIPATE OR KNOW. SO THE NEXT ROUND OF TESTING WILL INCLUDE APPLICATION OWNERS OR PERHAPS A SMALL GROUP OF TRAINED INDIVIDUALS THAT RECOGNIZE THAT THEY ARE NOT TO DISCUSS RESULTS WITH OTHER PEOPLE IN THE ORGANIZATION, BUT ARE GIVING FEEDBACK DIRECTLY TO THE ENGINEERS OR PRODUCT/PROJECT MANAGERS TO DETERMINE IF ITERATIVE CHANGES ARE REQUIRED. VALIDATION IS SOMETIMES REQUIRED IN NEAR-PRODUCTION TEST ENVIRONMENTS, BUT IF POSSIBLE, THE IT TEAM SHOULD TRY TO AVOID EXPOSING PRODUCTION DATA TO THIS TESTING PHASE. THE RISK HAS INCREASED BECAUSE YOU HAVE TYPICALLY INCREASED THE POPULATION OF TESTERS TO INCLUDE NON-IT INDIVIDUALS. FEWER CHANGES SHOULD BE TAKING PLACE DURING THIS PROCESS BECAUSE MORE USERS MAKE COMMUNICATION MORE DIFFICULT. SOME ENVIRONMENTS MAY REFER TO THIS STYLE OF TESTING AS "ALPHA" TESTING.

3. **PROOF OF CONCEPT**. THE GOAL OF THE PROOF OF CONCEPT IS TO SEEK MANAGEMENT AND STAKEHOLDER APPROVAL BASED ON PREVIOUSLY DEFINED SUCCESS CRITERIA. THE TIMEFRAME OR ORDER A PROOF OF CONCEPT (POC) IS CONDUCTED MAY VARY, BUT I FIND THAT IT IS BEST TO PERFORM BEFORE USER ACCEPTANCE TESTING (UAT) WHENEVER POSSIBLE. I LIKE TO CONTINUE TO AVOID EXPOSING THE ENVIRONMENT TO PRODUCTION USERS IF POSSIBLE, BUT OUR GOAL WILL BE TO PROVE TO THE STAKEHOLDERS THAT THE CHANGES HAVE A HIGH LIKELIHOOD OF SUCCESS IN PRODUCTION. IF THEY HAVE NOT BEEN INVOLVED IN VALIDATION TESTING, I HIGHLY ENCOURAGE YOU TO MAKE SURE SERVICE DESK MEMBERS ARE INVOLVED AT THIS POINT. THE REASON FOR THIS IS THAT OUR NEXT STEPS WILL INVOLVE USERS, AND TYPICALLY THEY WILL ENGAGE THE SERVICE DESK IF THEY RUN INTO ISSUES.

You want to avoid a service incident to be generated because you didn't prep the right teams. Remember, negative perceptions carry further than you think they will.

4. **UAT** (User Acceptance Testing). Now that changes have passed the eyes of those who know best- it is time to put the change into a near-production or pre-production environment and ask a pre-defined group of individuals (again, trained to give feedback) to work in the system, typically for a day or so. These people will perform their daily tasks or run a battery of tests. Again, the risk has increased because this group should be larger, about one to two percent of the user population. Remember, even less rapid changes can be done in this phase because you are asking a larger population to test with their day-to-day workflows. Another goal of the UAT process is to gather feedback on documentation if needed to communicate to users about what to expect.

5. **Pre-Production Pilot**. Now that stakeholders have approved the changes, it is time to schedule a rollout to a limited population of users- about 10 to 20 percent of the overall population. This lowers the risk of a complete outage in most cases and allows for work to continue in the event the changes need to be rolled back. I typically recommend between two weeks to two months of Pre-Production Pilot for major changes, but in some cases, this may be as little as a day. It should also be noted that even this process is not always possible in certain scenarios such as Healthcare software which often requires an 'all or nothing' change to software all at the same time. None the less- you should always strive to target a smaller population early on to lower the risk to the business.

6. **Production Rollout**. Once the pilot is successful and no further changes are required, it is time to make the change for everyone. Make sure your documentation is up to date and that support personnel are prepped. Communication across all teams, not just yours is essential at this step. You will likely experience the most stress on the first day of rollout, especially if it is done at night. The more you are ready for it by being properly prepared, the easier

IT WILL BE. WE WILL BE TALKING MUCH MORE ABOUT ASSURING PRODUCTION STABILITY IN THE MAINTAIN TOPIC.

7. **QUALITY ASSURANCE** (QA). LARGER OR MORE CRITICAL OPERATIONS MAY HAVE A DEDICATED ENVIRONMENT THAT MIRRORS PRODUCTION WITH THE EXPLICIT PURPOSE OF CRISIS MITIGATION, STRESS TESTING, SIZING SIMULATIONS AND LOAD TESTING. THIS ENVIRONMENT SHOULD BE UPDATED ONCE THE PRODUCTION ROLLOUT IS ENTIRELY SUCCESSFUL. PRODUCTION USERS SHOULD NOT BE PART OF THE QA ENVIRONMENT AS IT WILL OFTEN HAVE A DEDICATED ACTIVE DIRECTORY OR USER DATABASE STRUCTURE SO AS TO PROVIDE PROPER ISOLATION FOR LOAD TESTING. VERY OFTEN, A QA ENVIRONMENT WILL BE USED TO VALIDATE PERFORMANCE CHANGES BEFORE ROLLOUT INTO PRODUCTION OR TO TEST BREAK-FIX PATCHES RAPIDLY BY ADMINISTRATORS CHARGED WITH THE TASK.

8. **QA/TEST**. SOME ENVIRONMENTS WILL OPT TO HAVE A NON-ISOLATED QA ENVIRONMENT THAT IS EXPLICITLY USED FOR PATCH VALIDATION AND LIGHT IMPACT TESTING IN THE SAME ENVIRONMENT. THIS HAS THE BENEFIT OF ALLOWING THE ENGINEERING TEAMS TO CONTINUE DEVELOPMENT TESTING WITHOUT BEING INVOLVED IN PATCH TESTING OR HAVING TO MAINTAIN VERSION LEVELS IN THE DEV ENVIRONMENT. PATCH TESTING IS PERFORMED HERE THEN SENT TO UAT FOR VALIDATION. IN SOME ENVIRONMENTS, THIS VALIDATION IS AUTOMATED AND EVALUATED FOR IMPACTS BEFORE AUTOMATIC ROLLOUT. THERE ARE RISKS HERE, BUT IT CAN SAVE A LOT OF TIME AND IS BETTER TO HAVE SOME VALIDATION TESTING RUNNING THAN JUST DEPLOYING INTO PRODUCTION.

Key Hero Concept: Reduce Risk as Population Exposure Increases.

While I don't always recommend small changes go through this full process, the concept is that you're reducing risk as you increase population exposure to your change.

To demonstrate this, I'm pulling from the training I performed on this topic. You can get access to this training as part of the bonuses for this book at https://ctxpro.com/herobonus7

Here's how this looks from a number of users versus the amount of risk exposure:

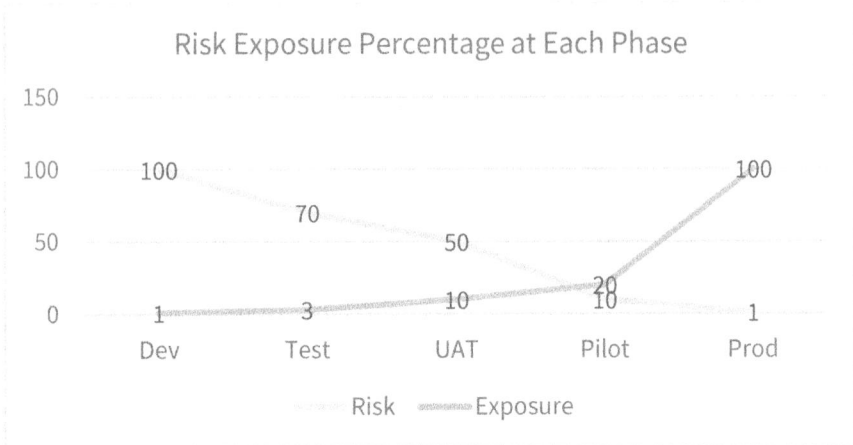

Figure 31: Risks at each phase and user exposure

We try to limit to only one percent or less of the population that ever see our development or testing level processes. For UAT, we may only expose the change to three percent of the overall user population, often first to application owners that can help us validate practically.

For Pilot, about 10% of the population for this because you're still at a pretty high-risk level the change might work, but you haven't put it through an actual workday.

If possible, once validated at this level for functionality, we'll run automated testing (such as LoginVSI) and make sure that it's not going to have any impact on the system that you need to know about before you put the change in front of users.

While at this point, our risks should drop dramatically, we still don't want to assume that we know that is not an indicator of trouble. The results for 10% do not necessarily indicate what we will see with all 100%. To combat this, we try to increase the number of users to about 10 to 20% during the pilot to fully validate the changes *before* rollout. At that level, the odds of risk have dropped to the point where a rollout to the large population has acceptable risk levels – remembering that nothing is ever assured 100% of the time.

Putting it all Together

Let's put this together using the Methodology!

Understand

Whether your targeted *Change* is something as simple as applying Windows updates, or there's a patch to the software, or it's a massive change like going from XenApp 6.5 to LTSR, defining the changes required and why it's happening are essential. Defining the success criteria is essential, no matter the change. This is an excellent habit to have, small as it may seem. If you get good at a small thing, then you can get good at a big thing.

In other words, instead of hoping that you'll rise to the occasion when there's a crisis, the reality is you won't rise to that occasion.

You will not rise to the occasion. You will only rise to the level of your preparedness.

If you get used to doing this process for small things, you'll be able to put it into place for big things as well much more easily. However, always make sure you're outlining potential risks, even if you don't know what they are.

Outlining Risks

If you don't know what the impacts of your change could be, that is a risk in and of itself! If you're running a patch (for example, it's Tuesday for Microsoft patches), you don't always know what those risks are reading the descriptions.

You could classify a few risks in this kind of situation. For example, your risk may be as simple as impacts on system performance. Or, they could be system stability. Or application compatibility. Until you test, you won't truly know, but you need to tune your mind and processes towards watching for these risks. If the answer is "I don't know what the risks are," that is an acceptable start, and you should be honest about that. But with a little thought, you can typically define potential impacts. Remember that often NOT applying an update is a risk.

Write the Plan

Next, you will Plan. Given what we know about the risks vs. benefits, outline whatever is going to happen and document it:

- What are the planned actions we are going to take to move this forward?
- What is our backout plan?
- What is our standard process for this?

Now you will be able to inform your Change Control meeting to be able to say:

"Here's our standard risk template for this sort of thing, and here's what we feel the plan should be."

It may seem pointless at times. But remember:

> *To be a hero, sometimes we have to protect people in ways they never knew we protected them.*

By being proactive with risks, we're doing just that. But we need to do the work. Get it in writing and get an agreed plan.

Change

Timeline

What gets missed many times in a lot of Change Control meetings is the timeline required. A good Change Control process will always ask: what is our anticipated timeline for start, in-process and completion? Additionally, defining an extended timeline, that is, how long can this process run before we call it an incident?

This is more important on significant system changes- but try to keep the amount of time you have scheduled doing it open as much as you can so that you're not under stress if things go a little badly. This means when you can, over-estimate the time required. I typically pad about 10% whenever I get a time estimate. I call those my "Scotty" moments. If you didn't watch Star Trek, you might not know what I'm talking about – but the thought is that a good engineer always overestimates the time so they can be seen as a miracle-worker. I may not endorse that part of the thinking, but to be a hero sometimes you have to exceed expectations!

The healthy thing here is that you aren't a villain if the time is exceeded because you gave extra time to get it done.

Communication

Take change control seriously and look at making sure you're getting everybody on board and communicating that properly as a big part of the planning process.

Testing

Next, we need to define the testers for each stage of the process, whether it be development within IT, including application owners or developers. We need to make sure everyone is okay with the changes, making sure user acceptance testing is part of that process.

Our next step is performing that first change in your Sandbox or Test environment within IT. Remember, our goal here is to make sure you are not doing anything that impacts production. So as far as users go, there's no awareness of anything changing at all (right now, anyway). *(Note: as I'm editing this chapter and reviewing the fact that I even felt compelled to write these sentences often pains me. Yet – nearly every client I visit having trouble seems to ignore this step. Please don't let that be you.)*

I say this from some bad experiences I've had or cleaned up after. I've seen standard Microsoft patching take down a PVS environment (therefore affecting everyone) more times than I can count. If the risk is that high, especially in those high-risk environments where it is Mission Critical that Citrix is working, it is essential to take this seriously. Isolate and validate those changes (no matter how simple or 'standard') first with IT, and then with the stakeholders. If there is an issue, this is where we go back into the process and re-evaluate the changes and make any changes; we try again.

Hero Moment: Counting the Cost

I often hear server admins complaining that it takes too much space, cycles or overhead to maintain a test environment. If you are facing resistance, have your management consider a few things:

1) *What was last year's cost of downtime caused by patches or changes we could have tested before deployment but couldn't because we don't have a test environment?*

2) *How much does it cost to have a test environment that doesn't have to run 24-7; that can be brought up and down when needed to validate changes?*

3) *Are we sure #2 is that much greater than #1?*

Whenever possible, I suggest you test with application owners in your test environment. This allows us to make sure we can pass through this process first with people we work with closely before we put this in front of anybody else. If at all possible, make sure these are people that you can trust to work with you and not against you!

We always expose the least amount of people in the organization possible to any risk.

I call this a pre user acceptance test. This is the part of the process where we validate these changes with the actual people that are going to be defining and tracking the success criteria. In other words, the people that are going to be saying, "This is what working looks like."

User Feedback

It is far better to get feedback at this point in the process. That is why we ask the question: Is there anything else we need to do to accomplish our goals?

Performance Testing

If things look good and no issues are reported, this is usually the point where I recommend doing some load testing - before we do any further rollout. Remember that perceptions of poor performance are often just as bad if not worse than if it's not working at all, at least in terms of what about which users will complain the most loudly.

If it's just a patch to a PVS vDisk, for example, that may not seem like a big deal in terms of impacts - but still needs to be something that you're communicating out as a change. This is because if somebody in your user acceptance testing is calling the help desk instead of you, the service desk desperately needs to know what's going on. It does happen. Even though they're told to call you if there's any changes or any problems and roll back to the previous process, people forget that people get busy. They are just trying to get their work done and have other habits.

Please understand this: Not every negative impact shows up in individual testing. I'm editing this in February 2020, and this week I got a panic call that everything was 'slow' in a relatively small PVS-imaged environment. I very quickly found that every single VM was spending the first 30 or so minutes after logon at 40% CPU. Usually, I would attribute this to a process called nGen that is typically queued after Windows Updates (we talked about way back in Chapter 1!) that in a non-persistent environment means that every boot it's the same process running over and over. In this case, add to that the Microsoft Anti-Malware scanner was running a full scan of the disks. So, CPU AND overrunning the network! Fortunately, PVS caches from RAM, so the impact was not as bad as it could have been (ahem!) but understand that in this case, they had deployed the update, tested it, and everything seemed okay. They had failed to notice the CPU. This is why I'm a fan of automated patch testing! If part of your process is always to validate even small changes like Windows Update don't impact performance – you'll avoid these potential pitfalls!

Communication

You need communication about said changes, even if only 10 percent of the population is targeted or impacted.

Make sure you arrange the validation testing time frames and that the Service Desk and other individuals in IT can report back to you with any feedback or whatever is needed there. Again – this seems like such a small thing, and all the time I see IT teams do these sorts of testing and changes without communicating to the broader team. And then, bad things happen. I have seen preventable escalations occur because the tester didn't correctly communicate what they were testing, or the service desk didn't know about the testing and assumed things were down. The temptation to consider these things low risk can create new risks!
Hero: follow a procedure!

Back-Out Plan

Regardless of your level of confidence with the changes, make sure you have a back-out plan. That preparation is something that gets missed often. It might seem simple to you. It may seem obvious to many. Just make sure you are stating what it is.

For example, in the event updates to a VDA image go poorly enough to justify a back-out, you can revert to the previous PVS or MCS image (or version). State in the change control form that this is our rollback plan. Make sure it is well documented regardless of how obvious it is. In the backout plan, be appropriate with how much time you think it'll need to be completed. The more prepared for these questions you are, the easier the Change Control meeting will be.

How much time will it require to recover?

What would the outage entail (especially user impacts like apps that users wouldn't be able to log into)? These are things that should be in communications to users before the change. If you don't know: overestimate instead of underestimate, but don't get ridiculous. Claiming the system will be down for a business day for what would encompass 4 hours to change and a back-out may cover you for additional time, but is likely not going to get the change approved. Or – the change request would be rescheduled for a time you don't want to work, such as nights or weekends.

Avoid drama!

Try whenever possible to include language like "based on our testing this is what the timelines look like" or something similar as appropriate.

Update Documentation

Once we've rolled those changes out and our testing goals have been met, we collect feedback, document, and briefly visit the Understand Phase to see if we need to make any design adjustments. We need to look at data from a performance perspective. This is where monitoring comes into play because it assures that what we assume is real.

Pilot and Production Rollout

Once we are sure our risks have been addressed in UAT/Validation testing, it is time to make your plan for your broader rollout. First, we deploy into a pilot. Next, the larger population into production. We roll out using the same kind of methods (read: it is second nature now that we have practiced!).

Communications

The big difference with a pilot (and then a production rollout) is the changes in our communications to at least leadership, but sometimes communication to users if they should expect changes, especially visually, that's usually when you need to update users. The beauty of using this method is that you'll know if that is going to be a requirement because you've already done the testing. You have already had users in your UAT exposed to this if there's any visual changes or things like that that they'd be concerned about they would have let you know so you can make screenshots.

Remember, an informed user is a happier user.

What you are communicating to the user is, "Here's what you'll need to expect and what you'll need to do if there are any action steps." From their point of view, this prevents the response to unexpected things that go on in the environment. In my observation, about 80% of the time or more, when users are exposed to unannounced visual or experience changes - they will throw up their hands (quit working). They will stop what they're doing and call the help desk because they've been instructed to do that.

Avoid the temptation to be frustrated with users that do that. Remember, if there's anything funny going on, the message they've been given is, "If you see something, say something." Especially when your system is very consistent from day to day. If something changes that they didn't expect, most people think it is a virus.

Hopefully, you can see it is vital to communicate with your users if changes are going on.

Keeping those communications into the right places and choosing a group of people that are going to be doing your pilot is imperative.

Pilot User Selection

Whom you select to be part of the Pilot is very important. You want to be strategic about who is part of the rollout, making sure that every use case and department has good representation in your overall pilot population. Arranging this to happen in advance is hugely effective at reducing the risks of having a poorly perceived rollout. The scenario of rolling back an entire change because of something that a single department sees is as palpable. Therefore, choose wisely.

135

In a pilot to production rollout, once the chosen (smaller) part of the population has been using the changes successfully, in almost all cases, you can bring the remaining 80% of the population in more rapidly. In the rollouts I have been a part of for the last eight years using this method – very rarely have additional risks surfaced once a representative 20 percent of the population has been using the change for a week. Meaning that the risk-to-benefit ratio is changed at that percentage of user population, so a slower rollout becomes detrimental. However, I caveat this with just because it has been rare doesn't mean it hasn't happened. So always be prepared – but always move forward with purpose.

> *Risk is part of the game if you want to sit in that chair.*
> *– James Tiberius Kirk (fictional)*

Maintain

We want to make sure we are monitoring for risks, and we always want to make sure that especially during the first few days of the rollout. We want to be paying careful attention to our monitoring to make sure that we do not see any performance degradation that we didn't expect. Also, during this time, the other thing that many would-be heroes miss is documenting the changes you made! Post-Pilot Rollout is the absolute best time to be doing this because you need to be present and attentive. However, if you've done your job well, your direct attention won't be needed which makes the perfect time to document while you "keep an eye on things!"

Documentation

You may have heard the internet-popular phrase – "Screenshot, or it didn't   happen."
Often the first thing we reach for in our minds when we are troubleshooting is, "well, what did it look like when it worked?" Future troubleshooting and changes are why perhaps a vital aspect of Change Management is to DOCUMENT YOUR CHANGES!

Document what went right, what went wrong. If you have the process documented and need to make changes down the road, don't rely on your memory. Having it written down can be hugely beneficial for management as well.

If you need another reason – here is a big one: When you need to prove a project needs more time than is being allocated, nothing beats pulling up documentation from 'last time.'

Or consider this a personal plea. As a consultant that is typically called in to assess and help troubled projects work – I can't make assumptions. I'm going to interrupt what you planned on doing that day to write down what you did previously. Having it written down for me will make your life easier.
The same goes for that new person that will inevitably be hired. You don't want to spend hours stopping what you are doing to explain what went on and why. Therefore, at a minimum, write a one-page summary of your processes with addendums for deployment notes. But if you want to be the hero- you can do better than that.

Do it for yourself. Writing quality documentation makes you *valuable*. I know very few Citrix Admins and Engineers that stay with the same company for their entire careers. Having demonstratable habits such as keeping documentation make you not only easy to hire – but appreciated after the fact by your former company. We are a small and tight community. Your replacement will appreciate you and speak well of you to others. It seems small, but **I believe that what I've laid out in this chapter and being willing to document it as a service to others has been the defining difference in my career**.

In Closing
And with that – I close this work. I set out with a goal three years ago to offer some helpful tips. This evolved into a "Top 3" blog, then a downloadable 20-page PDF. Now, this book has over 40,000 words! I hope that it has been helpful to you and that I've been able to give you just a few things that will help you be successful in your career.
If there's anything I can do for you to help you succeed, it is my hope to be able to either provide that or point you in the right direction. Feel free to contact me at CoachDJ@CTXPro.com. I have other books, courses, and other materials coming (if not already out by the time you're reading this). I'm passionate about inspiring the next generation of tech leaders.

Finally, a favor if you would. The best way you can help me improve, or if something is working to help me do more of it is to leave an HONEST review on Amazon about this book. This helps me to either write a better book next time or help someone else make the decision to read this one and help their career. Both are meaningful for me!

Creating work like this is now my profession; it is what is supporting my family. It is where my passions are. And, we can go deeper together, you and I! If you're interested, go to https://ctxpro.com or https://JustDoTHIS.net to find a training course or other material. I email discount codes to my email list as often as I can do so. Join the list or... just email me directly! I'm happy to get discount or access codes to those that ask when I have them available!

I appreciate your support in exchange for this training and perspective that took hundreds of hours to develop and then write down, edit, publish, and promote. Each book costs thousands of dollars to produce. So, I hope you will continue to support those that get the information to you in whatever that form comes!

Now go forth, Hero!

Leave IT Better Than You Found it!

-DJ Eshelman, March 2020

Appendix

The following are items that I had as part of the presentations I gave in my original Citrix Hero Program. These are from voice transcripts and notes that have not been edited quite as carefully. You can read them here, but honestly, I felt much of this was better delivered visually. Head to https://ctxpro.com/herobonus7 to register and get access to these training courses and presentations.

Being the Hero

These are some tips I often give to coaching clients and others asking me what it takes to set yourself apart from others in the IT world.

Planning Ahead

One key thing that will absolutely set you apart from the rest of your peers and terms of standing out to management for promotions, bonuses, et cetera, and that is planning ahead. Being Proactive. If you are the person that is doing these things, this will set you apart as a leader; someone who cares, and also somebody who is more likely to be up for that promotion. Be descriptive in ways that help other teams identify risk areas. Be upfront with people, especially in Change Control meetings. I find the term "sneak it in" within change control happening way too frequently. And so does your management. The problem with that mentality of 'sneaking it thru' is that it causes protectionism and isolation as far as one team not talking to the other. Not ideal, especially in the Citrix world.

If you find yourself doing that, remember – when we do that, it'll likely be done to us!

Make sure you are upfront about everything that is going on with a potential change and the potential risks that are there. Be descriptive about everything we're doing in the change. Other teams might have a change down the road that is affected by that or vice versa. There might be a change in the network that seems to them pretty minor.

"We're just going to change a helper address for our subnet. No big deal. Nothing the Citrix team needs to know."

Well, if you are running a PVS environment, for example, and that's the discussion that happens, and you don't catch that in a Change Control meeting – or because it was snuck in… That can cause an outage for your entire environment.

I say that because I've seen that happen more than three times in my career. That exact thing where something was just snuck into a change control or I think in one case it wasn't discussed in Change Control at all... It was just done! That's a different kind of resume generating opportunity entirely (that means they were fired in this case. They brought down the entire hospital system for 9 hours because the Citrix team didn't know about the change, and it made machines unable to boot).

Leave it Better Than You Found It

Remember: As Citrix Heroes, we want to leave it better than we found it. We genuinely want to act for the good of everyone we work with, even those you don't like. To be the hero, you still want to act in such a way that is for their benefit, even if they don't reciprocate. If you don't know what the risk is, you do need to say something like: "we don't have confidence as to if there are risks or not at this time." Far better than saying nothing at all, regardless of how uncomfortable it is.

Spending time lowering risk seems costly and may delay other projects. Spoiler alert: this is what working in IT is genuinely like.

Like Scotty on the Enterprise, sometimes you need to overestimate the efforts to give yourself room to make it work.

For production deployment, since you've gone through your process correctly, you should have an excellent idea of what risks could be present. You know how low the likelihood those risks will be. That is because we had already reduced risks before change control was ever even involved!

If there are significant issues after production rollout and you're using PVS (for example) – roll back the vDisk image to Test and reboot the VMs (personal note here, this is why I love PVS. What would be a massive outage while 2000 VMs are rolled back to a previous version becomes... a reboot over lunch.)

I hear you thinking: "But what if there was an issue identified during, say UAT testing? Aren't there still risks there? Won't people still freak out?"

But if UAT was done as I recommend, only about 200 of 2000 users were potentially even aware of the problem, and because you have a side by side process with those UAT users, they were able to go right back to work as if it weren't there. Psychologically, this feels safe. You have not made them victims – in fact, you've made THEM heroes because they have identified an issue that the population was shielded from. They may have just saved your job. Make sure to send them a thank you note.

Possibly more importantly for you: They weren't telling everybody they know how awful Citrix is because they just were able to go back to work and bounces right off of them.

It sounds like a great idea until it is done poorly, and you don't actually do any testing, or trust automation too much. I see it all too frequently in the field. When your automation does a new patch, roll it out, and you don't ever validate it or touch it, then you've got a problem. Less work, sure. You're busy – I get it. But I've seen far too many people get NO work done because of things like this. Don't take the risk. Take every change seriously.

On Automation

Automate testing, not impact. Use the tools available to make life easier by automating the right things. For example, Citrix AppDNA can automatically test software updates for compatibility issues before you put them in front of users. LoginVSI provides options for automated testing that can alert you when an application behaves differently than it had previously.

But if you try to automate outside of the guidance I've given you here – I'm going to deny I knew thee.

Automation Isn't Always Ideal

An incident that comes to mind was an automated roll out to what seemed simple Microsoft patches that nobody caught, and nobody knew how to do anything about anyway. Along with their automation was a bad practice that may be familiar to some of you: no documentation of the process. It was all in the admin's head.

Oh, did I mention the admin was on vacation at the time?

The system was down for two days, costing them cash in the business, about $250,000. In just two days of being down, it cost the company more than the person's salary and benefits for two years. It can happen. The admin came back and was met at the door by security. Coming back from vacation looking for a job just because of this one thing doesn't sound ideal. I'm all for automation of low-risk changes. Don't get me wrong. The IT and UAT processes, sure. Automate them. But you never really know the actual impacts of an outage until after it has occurred. I'd rather be the hero then somebody that's looking for another job because they cut corners to "get more done."

Remember:

You never really know the real impacts of an outage until after it has occurred. So avoid them by putting in the extra work if you know the changes would affect users. Or put more simply – think of others before yourself. That concept has survived the ages, and you will see that pattern in the successful in the world.

Authors Note: In the online membership course "Become a Citrix Hero" I went into more detail on some examples, including the previous one I was talking about of the Server 2016 migration and how it could have happened and how it did happen side by side. Initially, I thought about having the whole story here in the book but it was making the chapter unreasonably long. The full lesson will be available as a free bonus at https://ctxpro.com/herobonus7. Making cuts is hard. Now I know how Peter Jackson must have felt.

Real World Examples for Change Control

(In the final chapter, we talked about a scenario gone wrong. Let's look at how it could have gone right)

For a simple example, let's use a Windows 10 PVS image that requires a VDA Cumulative Update patch. We first have a few Understand and Plan tasks.

- *What are the patches to be applied?* LTSR 7.15 CU5 (7.15.5000)
- *Identify the risks and benefits of these patches*. Risks include negative performance impacts, being unable to establish a connection with the VDA, et cetera. Benefits include a cumulative rollup of more than 200 industry-driven stability fixes and extending support.
- *Identify where it will be applied and who will be exposed to the changes*. The Windows 10 IT Production Image will be first affecting 15 users. Next, 20 UAT users will validate the change. Once successful,

the changes will be rolled into the standard production image affecting 2000 users.

I will use as an example, a company with a simple QA/TEST style operation. Production changes happen first against a copy of the production vDisk that can be promoted directly to production if validated (Recall that new development happens in a separate DEV environment). In the PVS Console, they create a new maintenance version of the vDisk and boot the Maintenance VM (which is appropriately configured as a 'Maintenance' VM and, therefore, boots from the maintenance vDisk version). The new VDA update is applied, and the standard procedure to seal the disk is performed. Back in the PVS Console, the image is promoted to Test.

In this environment, impact testing is automated. Tools from LoginVSI validate automatically that the changes do not have noticeable impacts on the Test VMs.

Next, the IT group begins validation. The IT VMs are designated as 'Test' VMs in PVS and are rebooted. For the next two days, the team performs normal operations and notes any issues. If there are issues, the version is rolled back to maintenance, and the VMs rebooted to boot from the prior version.

Some changes may require validation from the *stakeholders*. There is predefined scheduling so that UAT testers knew in advance that this was coming, and the next day they knew that they would be on the UAT desktop, validating their workflow for the entire day. In this particular case, UAT users are allowed access to both the Production and UAT desktops. If they had any problems, all they had to do was go back to the other desktop they had in front of them. The UAT machines are booted, and the delivery group re-activated so that it appears as an option for the UAT group. They were instructed to use the UAT Desktop for the whole day to make sure the processes typically followed in production work properly. If anything was wrong, they were instructed to stop and go back to report the feedback to IT. In a majority of cases like this, there's usually no feedback. The reality is that most patch issues would have been identified. But again, that's no reason to take that risk!

Once the changes are all approved, the vDisk is promoted to Production. Upon the next reboot of the VMs, the change is automatically "applied".

This means that responsibility for assuring that it was done correctly doesn't just lean on you, nor did the risk.

Team Dynamics

I wanted to include a few more things about working with a team. This is taken from a few presentations I've given, and I hope it's helpful to you!

Getting the Whole Team Involved

The entire team really needs to be involved and onboard for reducing risks. Say you have one part of the team that is adopting a minimum viable product kind of thing and you're just going with a broken DevOps model of "we'll fix it later when we are less busy if people complain."

Resistance to the Model

Now say you want to adopt the strategy I note in the Change Management chapter. It's not impossible, but it can be challenging when these two philosophies clash. By the way – I consider DevOps a philosophy, not a method. This is often why when you present a strategy against a line of thinking, there can be friction.

If that means you need to go to upper management and plead your case, then I'm hoping that I've given you some material to do just exactly that thing. If enough interest is expressed, I have thought about making a presentation available that you'll be able to share with management.

If your management team is resistant to this or if it seems like a waste of time, start with the risk graph in chapter 7.

Tell them, "This is why we need to do this. We need to reduce the number of risks to which users are exposed. Doing this in a smart way, we're isolating production until it's very well tested."

There needs to be an investment in providing this isolation, so management needs to understand and 'buy-in' to the concept.

Resistance to a Sandbox/Dev Environment

If there is resistance to having a dedicated sandbox or an isolated lab, keep in mind that there is often commodity hardware when upgrades happen. Many times there's server hardware that has been purchased, but it's not really production stable anymore. It's not supported, but it's still there. These are good fits for making a lab, so stick your hand up and say, "If we've got these servers coming off, we'd like to have those for a lab."

Differences in Communications

Communicating with testers is crucial, as we've said. Be as transparent as possible about what is going on. If you can be good at communicating with them regularly, they'll be more likely to communicate with you in a crisis in a way that's helpful instead of just lousy perception.

Don't take shortcuts when it comes to communicating with your team. I've stepped into rooms with people yelling at each other because things have gone bad, usually because of shortcuts that were taken to "avoid drama."

I hear IT managers say that too often that "I'm working for them," and I "just need to get it done." Here's a tip. I've often had to come back on them and say, "We can do this, but there's so much risk that I have to have you   sign   this   waiver."
In consulting engagements, this is often called a Risk Memo. This memo or waiver communicates the risk and that they were aware of the risk and making the instruction to continue. If this is not possible- I'll remind you that IT jobs are among the easiest to find. Move along. Seriously. You'll bring the stress home in a situation where you are dealing with unreasonable people. There are others out there that believe in their people. If you have to move your family to find them, at least you'll come home happy to your family. But never believe that you are 'stuck' with a bad manager.

All that said, one thing I've noted about people that go it alone and operate outside of the team is that they are looking for work more often than they should be. Management and team buy-in is essential. Compromises are important. I always like to say that when kids don't have discipline, they usually grow up to be jerks. The same kind of thing is true with IT departments, if there's no discipline within the IT department they just kind of do whatever they feel like, they usually tend to be kind of jerks. Those are not generally people well received in the wider organization. Don't be that person.

Stakeholders

You want to make sure you have stakeholders that are identified in your projects that will challenge you. Sneaking changes in so you don't get

145

challenged seems like a good idea until something goes wrong and you get the finger pointed at you. What you want is a stakeholder who is accustomed to the finger being pointed at them that is going to actually challenge you on changes and make sure they are good for everyone.

Believe me that if you can put yourself into those people's radars, so to speak, it is beneficial for your career. Those stakeholders are the ones that are paying attention to who in the organization is ready to move up. You want people to be paying attention to the excellent work you're doing! Identify those people that will challenge you appropriately. You can answer them appropriately! The better you get at that confidence, the better you generally tend to be in your career.

Champion Users

Outside of this, whenever possible, get champion users involved that have observed how the process is done and make sure that you are connecting those people that have observed it go well. People like that can speak to the risks involved more completely. Be sure that the stakeholders that I just mentioned are connected with your champions so they can communicate with each other.

When the Manager Doesn't Agree

Some Managers push for something to be done that has too much risk. In cases like that, you need to push back when there are risks. Always remember that it is better to lose a job from a bad manager than to take the risk and 'just do it' badly. Here's the thing. If management is pushing you to take risks you aren't comfortable with – *they will still blame you when it goes badly*. "They told me to!" may feel good to say… but you are refreshing your resume regardless. Sorry to be so blunt, but I have to tell you – there are other jobs out there. Be Superman, not Batman. You want the people with you, not against you.

Make a plan to make sure everybody understands the process and get stakeholders involved in the meetings. Have pretty graphs for management and inform people who will be involved as to what change is going to look like.

Determine ways management can reward your testers for taking on the risks. It may be as simple as making testers first to get new hardware during a refresh or refreshed more frequently. It's the little things like that

that often make the difference of people being with you or not caring. Scratch their back so they can scratch yours, as the saying goes.

The Five Words that Kill

What you need to avoid saying (that I have observed in many change control meetings) is this phrase:

"It's fine. We tested it."

Don't do that even if you have spent time in front of users with it. Your stakeholders may be foolish enough to believe you. What you want here is a stakeholder to *speak on your behalf* having worked with you to assure the solution has merit. This has a far more powerful message and taps into something unspoken but true: If you get someone in the habit of speaking positively for you, that is a habit that repeats itself in other areas. Like, performance reviews, for example.

List of Web Links

The following is the list of links as of March 27th 2020. Please see https://ctxpro.com/CHlinks for updates to this list.

#	Link	Notes
1	https://community.citrixhero.com	Our Community Site!
2	https://docs.microsoft.com/en-us/windows-server/remote/remote-desktop-services/rds-vdi-recommendations	Microsoft VDI Optimizations
3	https://www.loginvsi.com/resources/white-papers/windows-server-2016-impact-on-vdi-benchmark-results	LoginVSI Server 2016 Benchmark
4	https://support.citrix.com/article/CTX224676	Citrix Optimizer
5	https://docs.citrix.com/en-us/smart-tools/checks/about-health-checks	Citrix Health Checks
6	https://www.carlstalhood.com/pvs-master-device-preparation/#tdsoftware	Carl Stalhood – PVS tweaks
7	https://www.loginconsultants.com/en/news/all/item/base-image-script-framework-bis-f	BIS-F

#	Link	Notes
8	https://labs.vmware.com/flings/vmware-os-optimization-tool/	VMware OST
9	https://www.bitdefender.com/files/News/CaseStudies/study/174/Bitdefender-Citrix-Hypervisor-Introspection-SolutionBrief.pdf	Hypervisor Introspection with XenServer
10	https://docs.citrix.com/en-us/tech-zone/build/tech-papers/antivirus-best-practices.html	Citrix Tech Zone: AntiVirus Recommendations
11	http://winhelp2002.mvps.org/hosts.htm	Hosts File
12	https://docs.citrix.com/en-us/xenapp-and-xendesktop/7-15-ltsr/citrix-vdi-best-practices.html	VDI Handbook
13	https://support.citrix.com/article/CTX216252	Citrix Windows 10 Optimization Guide
14	https://virtualfeller.com/2017/04/11/windows-server-2016-optimizations-for-citrix-xenapp/	Daniel Feller's 2016 Optimizations
15	http://pablolegorreta.com/windows-8-server-2012-optimization-guide/	Windows 8 thru Server 2012 R2 Optimizations
16	https://support.citrix.com/article/CTX123782	Enabling LDAP authentication
17	https://ctxpro.com/are-people-mining-bitcoin-on-your-netscaler-adc-using-cve-2019-19781/	DJ's Warnings on CVE 2019-19781
18	https://ctxpro.com/citrix-adc-remediation-cve-2019-19781/	Resolution Steps for CVE-2019-19781
19	https://ctxpro.com/best-ssllabs-com-netscaler-rating-vpx/	2016 Best Practices for NetScaler getting an A+ Rating
20	https://ctxpro.com/netscaler-security-pt1-assess/	2017 NetScaler Security practices lesson
21	https://www.citrix.com/blogs/2018/05/16/scoring-an-a-at-ssllabs-com-with-citrix-netscaler-q2-2018-update/	2018 Citrix Article on A+ rating

#	Link	Notes
22	https://support.citrix.com/article/CTX123680 and https://support.citrix.com/article/CTX123680	Disable SSL Regeneration and Enable HSTS
23	https://blog.qualys.com/ssllabs/2017/09/26/google-and-mozilla-deprecating-existing-symantec-certificates	Why there's a T Rating
24	https://support.citrix.com/article/CTX121149	NetScaler Leading Practices
25	https://support.citrix.com/article/CTX126736 and https://support.citrix.com/article/CTX111531	Lock down NetScaler Interfaces
26	https://en.wikipedia.org/wiki/Man-in-the-middle_attack	About Man in the Middle attacks
27	https://support.citrix.com/article/CTX200415 and https://ctxpro.com/securing-citrix-broker-xml-service-without-iis/	Securing XML traffic
28	https://www.citrix.com/blogs/2017/03/20/citrix-scalability-the-rule-of-5-and-10/	The Rule of 5 and 10
29	https://www.loginvsi.com/blog/834-influence-of-power-management-on-vdi-performance	Power Management Matters
30	https://helgeklein.com/blog/2013/05/the-effects-of-power-savings-mode-on-vcpu-performance/	Helge proved in 2013 that BIOS settings matter!
31	https://www.cisco.com/c/en/us/solutions/collateral/data-center-virtualization/unified-computing/whitepaper-c11-737931.html	Cisco UCS article about optimizing for virtualization
32	https://support.citrix.com/article/CTX125126, https://www.citrix.com/blogs/2012/10/25/pvs-internals-1-cache-manager/ and https://www.citrix.com/blogs/2013/07/03/pvs-internals-2-how-to-properly-size-your-memory/	Dan Allen's original article, Martin Zugec on sizing RAM
33	https://www.citrix.com/blogs/2018/09/05/pvs-internals-4-vdisk-stores-and-smb3/	Can you store PVS vDisk stores on SMB Shares?
34	https://blogs.technet.microsoft.com/grouppolicy/2013/05/23/group-policy-and-logon-impact/	Microsoft on Group Policy and logon impact

149

#	Link	Notes
35	https://james-rankin.com/articles/make-citrix-logons-use-asynchronous-user-group-policy-processing-mode/ and https://docs.microsoft.com/en-us/previous-versions/windows/it-pro/windows-server-2012-r2-and-2012/dn581922(v%3Dws.11)	James Rankin on Async GPP and Microsoft on GPP
36	https://www.youtube.com/watch?v=54Y7gdhc0mU	Hal Lange Demonstrates WEM System Optimization
37	https://www.carlstalhood.com/workspace-environment-management https://www.jgspiers.com/citrix-workspace-environment-manager/ https://www.christiaanbrinkhoff.com/2017/06/09/how-to-configure-citrix-workspace-environment-management43-for-xenapp-or-xendesktop https://docs.citrix.com/en-us/workspace-environment-management/current-release https://jkindon.com/2019/01/02/wem-hydration-kit-module-environmental-settings-to-registry-actions/ https://deyda.net/index.php/en/tag/administration-console-en/	My WEM Bookmarks

Thank You and Acknowledgements

Thank you for reading this book. I hope it is something you found useful and will someday pay it forward by creating content of your own to equip and encourage our community. If you are interested in submitting content for publication on the Citrix Hero or Citrix Professionals site, we would be very interested in you doing so! Please contact us at support@ctxpro.com

Now – it's your turn. I'm challenging you to be a Citrix Hero! Please share what you've learned in an Amazon review, or share this book on Social Media using #CitrixHero. If we don't share our stories, they are of no help to anyone! Feel free to use https://ctxpro.com/book to point people toward this book- that is a permanent link!

I would like to take a moment and thank so many of my community members that have been patient in waiting for this work to be completed.

Of course, thank you to Citrix for your products and for taking a chance on me. I wouldn't be where I am today had I not begun working with Citrix Consulting in 2011.

Thank you to the CTA and CTP members I have had the pleasure of serving with over the past three years, and of course to the Citrix User Group Community.

Thank you to my wife Yvette and her patience and support, and for believing in me when I didn't.

I'd like to also thank the members of my Citrix Hero community for their support.

Also a very special thanks to our Book Launch Team, who helped proofread this book!

But most of all I thank God for the gift of life and for inspiring my breath, my words and my vision. The gifts I have been given are all to God's credit and glory!

About the Author

DJ Eshelman lives in the Nashville, TN area (USA). While not creating books and training material to equip professionals with what they need to be successful, he occasionally still serves as an independent consultant for Citrix Consulting and other organizations. He has served companies of all sizes, including 20 of the Forbes Top 100 companies.

- Citrix Certified Expert (CCE-V)
- CTA (Citrix Technology Advocate) 2017-2019

- CUGC Leader – Founded Colorado Chapter in 2016. Co-Lead Nashville from 2017-2020
- Creator of CTXPro.com
- CitrixCoach.com – Creator & Lead Coach
- Resident Consultant with Citrix Consulting Services

DJ is a Life and Career Coach and is a firm believer that to be most successful we must have the attitude of leaving the world better than we found it. He recently began a podcast network at BTYFI.net.

This work is not intended to diagnose, guide or prescribe specific actions for your environment. Any information is given as-is and subject to change. This work is not affiliated in any way with Citrix Systems nor its affiliates or partners. You are encouraged to verify and validate any information given before making any production changes. Where appropriate, internet links are provided to help you make informed decisions.

If you are unsure or need further help, I encourage you to reach out to me at CoachDJ@CTXPro.com to see if coaching or consulting sessions are appropriate.

All copyrights mentioned in this work are the property of their creators and are referenced for educational purposes only, not as an endorsement or call to purchase.